CASTLE COMBE
CIRCUIT
the first 50 years

By
Paul Lawrence and Peter Stowe

Foreword by
Sir Stirling Moss OBE

tfmPublishing Limited

Published by:-

t*f*m **Publishing Limited**
Brimstree View
Kemberton
Nr. Shifnal
Shropshire
TF11 9LL

Tel: 01952 586408
Fax: 01952 587654
E-mail: nikki@tfmpub.freeserve.co.uk

Design and layout: Nikki Bramhill

First Edition   June 2000

ISBN 1 903378 00 1

Printed by Frontier Print and Design Limited
Pickwick House
Chosen View Road
Cheltenham
Gloucestershire
GL51 9LT

Tel: 01242 573863
Fax: 01242 511643

Contents

Foreword

I was very pleased to be invited to write a foreword for this book covering the first 50 years in the history of Castle Combe. It is undoubtedly largely due to the unstinting efforts of Howard and Pat Strawford that the circuit has not only survived those 50 years, but also reached a position as one of the busiest venues in British motor sport.

I have rather happy memories of competing at Castle Combe during my early career. I scored several 500cc Formula 3 victories there but also had a pretty nasty accident in October 1953 when Tony Rolt in Rob Walker's Connaught clipped my Cooper from behind and sent me rolling at Quarry Corner. I had a night in a Bristol hospital with a broken shoulder as a result!

However, that aside I am delighted to join in the celebrations of 50 years of the circuit. Without venues like Castle Combe, the sport would be much the poorer and I have every confidence that the work that Howard and Pat have done will ensure that the circuit goes on to make its first century. The on-going improvements make Castle Combe a great place to visit, whether as a racer or fan, and I wish everyone involved an excellent 50th birthday celebration.

Sir Stirling Moss

London
April 2000

Introduction

Developing a parkland feel for the circuit has always been one of Strawford's priorities.

Photo: Trevor Porter.

Castle Combe Circuit was originally part of the Castle Combe estate owned by Sir John Gorst. He died in 1916 without a son and heir and the estate was managed through trustees by a Chippenham firm of solicitors. After the second World War, the estate was broken up and sold.

The circuit was opened by his daughter, who I only knew as Mrs Kay Thomas, in conjunction with friends from the Bristol Motor Cycle & Light Car Club. But as the break up of the estate suggests, it was a low budget effort.

The halcyon days of the early 50's, including Formula 1 and Formula 2 races, were soon shattered by the 1955 Le Mans disaster and the ensuing new safety measures, which were to prove too expensive. The track closed for car racing and became a mecca for motorcycle racing plus lots of sprints and high speed trials.

It reopened for car racing in 1962 when the safety system was funded by the BRSCC, which started life as the 500 Club in the West Country, mainly by British Aeroplane Company staff, with 500cc racing being a regular feature at all early meetings.

Circuit owners AFN's application to achieve permanent planning permission, needed to fund an urgent resurfacing of the entire track, was rejected. An appeal was lost restricting racing to only 21 days per annum with closure by the end of 1971.

Stirling Moss during his accident in October 1953.

Photo: LAT.

The village was transformed for the filming of Dr. Doolittle, which featured the acting talents of commentator Andy Blackman as an extra.

Simultaneously, the Doctor Doolittle film was made in the village, renamed Puddleby-on-the-Marsh for the occasion. 20th Century Fox restored the village to its former glory, taking out all TV aerials and advertising signs.

The area was designated an Area of Outstanding Natural Beauty, which was to make planning matters much harder. This despite five other UK circuits being located in AONBs, including Brands Hatch.

John Webb's MCD (Motor Circuit Developments) sublet the circuit, promising to sort out the planning and bring the best of national motorsport. The latter they definitely achieved from Formula 3 and Formula Atlantic to the spectacular Formula 5000.

Peter Gethin won the Formula 5000 race on aggregate in May 1970.

Photo: Ferret Fotographics.

Temporary permission was again sought in 1971, tied in with AFN's new owners Porsche GmbH's search for a new import centre with test track. Five days motor racing each year was applied for and granted, but nothing else. Unable to survive on this level of usage, the company was sold to us.

Some very small activities started with a slowly slowly catchie monkey programme. In 1980 temporary planning was won on appeal to open a racing school. Castle Combe Racing School was born, initially just training and testing days, going on to run fun days for novices. In 1982 permanent planning permission was obtained, as usual in appeal, utilising the services of James Hunt as an expert witness. Frankly he was brilliant, displaying his remarkable knowledge, intelligence and splendid wit.

Following protracted negotiations with Forrester & Forrester in 1985, I managed to purchase the freehold of the circuit from the estate, with Mrs Thomas' active support. In 1988, further land came onto the market allowing the circuit to buy the land around the back of the circuit. This offered the opportunity to open up the Old Paddock/Hammerdown area for spectators and also develop the Old Paddock area into a skid pan, kart track and 4WD centre. In 1990, the circuit acquired the only unused piece of land from the Upper Castle Combe part of the estate, the land in the centre of the track.

Further planning battles in the '90s took the usage to over 250 days, albeit mainly road silenced vehicles, including 12 race days, sprints, racing school and motorcycle track days. The company also diversified into car boot sales, classic runs, action days, usage by the Under 17s Car Club, biathlons and lots of cycle racing.

In the mid '90s, all the former wartime buildings were extensively revamped in the new corporate image that the track had developed, plus the ageing Avon Tyres pedestrian bridge was replaced with a new one, fully Health and Safety compliant.

The Avon Bridge is one of the best known Castle Combe landmarks.

Subsequently six new toilet blocks have been built in the public areas, giving the circuit the best facilities of any national circuit in Britain. In the mid-1990s, the circuit was named the most neighbour and visitor friendly circuit in the UK.

In 1999, four new corners were added in the first configuration change since the circuit first opened. The track length was extended a little to 1.85 miles. The previous lap record was held by Nigel Greensall (Formula 1 Tyrrell 022) at 50.59 seconds; 130.93mph.

The new configuration circuit record is held currently by Bob Light in his B6 Sport at 1m03.389s (105.07mph). In the year 2000, the circuit celebrates its 50th anniversary.

Owning a circuit makes you a jack of all trades. It might be a struggle to learn about advertising, public relations and promotion, but if you've been a salesman you've got a fair idea. But that doesn't prepare you for putting up armco and building cess pits. It certainly doesn't prepare you for dealing with legal matters about planning law! However I scored heavily on this front by teaming up with Martin Chick a senior lecturer on planning at the University of the West of England.

Who would have predicted 25 years ago that now we would be operating over 250 days per annum, employing circa 25 people full time, 100 part time and generating £15m into the local economy. A dream come true.

Howard Strawford
Castle Combe Circuit
May 2000

Chapter 1

Castle Combe estate
and
the wartime airfield

The second world war changed many things for many people. In rural Wiltshire, it signalled the beginning of the end for the Castle Combe Estate, a baronial estate that had survived for 850 years. But as the war clouds gathered over Europe, the possibility of this area of productive farm land eventually becoming one of Britain's most popular race circuits was inconceivable.

Lying in the parish of Upper Combe to the west of Chippenham, the area comprised mainly flat agricultural land. The village sited in a wooded valley, originally called Under Combe, became known as Castle Combe

after the Normans built a castle. Local quarries provided building stone for the village.

The Castle Combe Estate was owned by the Scrope family for nearly 500 years, until it was purchased in 1896 by Lancashire businessman Edward Chaddock Lowndes. In order to claim an inheritance he had changed his name from the family name of Gorst. Reports of the day told that he acquired the entire village and nearly the whole parish of Castle Combe along with a considerable section of the parishes of Nettleton and Yatton Keynell. Upon his death in 1909, the estate passed to his brother Sir John Gorst. Having lived for six years in New Zealand and later been both a barrister and a Conservative MP, Gorst was to be one of the founders of the Liberal party.

His eldest son, Eldon, had been born in New Zealand but Sir John would out-live his son who died at the age of 50 in 1911. Sir Eldon Gorst worked for the Egyptian Government before

Castle Combe village, one of the prettiest in England.

Photo: Paul Lawrence

1

the turn of the century and was 42 when he married Evelyn Rudd from Argyll in 1903. They had a daughter, Katherine Rachael, who was born in 1905. She hated being called Katherine and would be widely known as Kitty until the late 1960s when she changed it once again to Kay.

When Sir John Gorst died in 1916, the estate passed into trust. Although Sir John had re-married in 1914, his second wife Ethel Johnson suffered poor health. But the estate could not pass to Kitty as she was not old enough at the time and it remained in trust until her grandmother-in-law finally passed away in 1969. 'It went into trust with solicitors running it, which was a disaster,' said Howard Strawford, later to be saviour of the venue for motorsport.

But in 1940, motorsport was out of the question as Europe went to war. Like so much of the farm land of the south of England, the area around Castle Combe soon attracted interest from the Air Ministry and part of the estate was quickly requisitioned for the construction of an airfield. At the same time, the Manor House was requisitioned by the Air Ministry as an RAF hospital.

At the outbreak of war, the area requisitioned was being farmed by Fred Kelly of Kents Bottom Farm and his father-in-law. After the airfield was built, Kelly continued to cut the grass for hay for his dairy herd.

The impact of the airfield on the small community was considerable and even away from the immediate airfield are lasting marks of the RAF. In Upper Combe is the collection of houses known as Whitegates. The original buildings here formed the main domestic site of the RAF camp, comprising hutted accommodation, messes, a gymnasium and the NAFFI. It was a typical dispersed domestic site, built around half a mile to the north-west of the airfield.

Amongst the buildings constructed on the main airfield was an Anderson hangar adjacent to what is now Old Paddock corner. The modern day offices and Bridgestone building were originally used as the maintenance unit and station armoury, the Tavern Clubhouse housed gas clothing, a respirator store and workshop while the scrutineering bay was a trailer and tractor store. The original control tower would later become race control.

RAF Castle Combe operated as a satellite of the larger Hullavington airfield and initially accommodated No.9 SFTS. This was a training unit for single-engine aircraft pilots, flying Oxford Trainers, Master I/IIs and Hurricanes. During the summer months Castle Combe proved very satisfactory, but with the onset of winter it was a different story. The grass surface soon became waterlogged and was unusable for long periods.

'It was an RAF training station and to this day I'm delighted it wasn't an operational station because it never gave us the massive runways that look so ugly everywhere else. It also makes it a much smaller site. It was a satellite station where they trained the Air Forces of the British Empire,' says Strawford. 'Mrs Thomas told me on one occasion that the New Zealand Air Force's headquarters in the UK were her old house, the Manor House.'

Despite the problems of waterlogged ground, the airfield continued to be used for pilot training and the laying of a Sommerfield track runway as well as construction of the perimeter track made the airfield usable once more. Indeed, the layout of the perimeter track would dictate the line of the race circuit after the war, although it did not follow the original plan.

'When they built the perimeter track, the original plan was to go straight into Quarry Corner, but the quarry came out where the circuit is now. They were infilling and infilling, but the war was on and so they stopped trying to fill the quarry and built the perimeter road with a kink in it. That's why Quarry Corner has such a unique shape. They filled in quite a lot of it, but ultimately, they had to stop and just build the track,' recalls Strawford.

Although relatively small, it was a busy site and by 1944 housed as many as 1200 RAF and WRAF personnel in an array of temporary buildings scattered around the main control tower. Perhaps the most action that Castle Combe saw during the war came one day in March 1944. A Stirling carrying five magnetic mines force-landed. Two of the mines exploded causing serious damage to a number of buildings. It was three days

The original airfield in 1946.

before training could restart using temporary accommodation.

Despite the use of foam slag and regrading the runways, the Sommerfield tracking still proved to be troublesome throughout 1944 and it was not until March 1945 that the airfield became fully serviceable, just as the war ended in Europe.

Ted Cowling was Flight Commander in 1945 and remembers the VE Day celebrations. 'All the members of the station celebrated VE Day with a colossal bonfire

next to the Airmen's mess and an all-ranks dance that evening in the same mess. I remember very well visiting all the pubs in Castle Combe village that evening in my MG with Joy, my fiancée. There were about six or seven airmen lying in the boot of the car, some were sitting on the roof and others were standing on the back seat with their heads out of the sunshine roof trying to shoot the cock off the church tower with a .22 rifle!'

'We disbanded towards end of August 1945 and flew to Brize Norton. I was then asked to fly four airmen back to Castle Combe as certain offices needed tidying up.

'This made me the last RAF pilot to land and take-off from RAF Castle Combe,' adds Cowling.

The station was then unoccupied until July 1946 when it was taken over briefly as a resettlement camp for Polish ex-servicemen. They occupied the huts until June 1948 when Castle Combe airfield closed and was disposed of in September. But the huts at Whitegates were soon taken over by post war homeless squatters. The site was later purchased by the local authority and the wartime huts were replaced by pre-fab houses. In 1960 the present houses were built.

The memorial plaque in the paddock.

Photo: Paul Lawrence

Long before the start of war, Kitty Gorst had proven herself a formidable and forward thinking lady. In 1927, at the age of 22, she married her first husband, William Lysley. In the 1930s, she showed her love of motor cars by competing on a number of rallies and trials. She was a member of the Womens' Automobile and Sports Association as well as the local Bristol Motor Cycle and Light Car Club. She tackled the RAC Rally at least twice during the 1930s in Rileys and contested trials throughout the region. Before the war she regularly attended races at Brooklands and Donington, although there is no record of her actually taking part in races.

Strawford was, and remains, a firm fan. 'Her wedding was one of the social events of the year. I will say now that I won't have a word said against her. You know, I had the most respect for the lady. She was one of the aristocracy, and she was educated in numerous languages and a desperately intelligent woman. She was a formidable lady and she was an enormous fan of technology.

'She was married three times. The first time was to William Lysley and as a result of that they went to live in what they call Shrub House. That is an enormous, rather serious, harsh-looking, cold house which is very, very hidden in Castle Combe. She lived there until her own son had children and then she decided she was rattling round in this old place. In the early fifties she had a Canadian cedar wood house built just down at the end of the village. Everyone thought she was mad but she liked new technology and I really liked the place.

'She never actually lived in the Manor House. They spent a fortune on constructing the garden there, including a formal Italian garden which survived and can still be seen at the hotel. She lived in Switzerland before the war and spent a lot of time there, having planned to build a house when funds permitted. However, she came back here and, I believe, married the estate manager soon after the war, a chap called Maurice,' reckons Strawford. Later still she would become Mrs Thomas through her third marriage.

The war years had not been kind to the Castle Combe Estate, though some would suggest that its problems were more to do with poor management during years in trust. By 1947 the estate was in a perilous financial position.

The potential costs of property repairs to near derelict buildings and the on-going support of Evelyn Gorst in the Bath Clinic led to the sale by auction of all the properties in the village. Held in Chippenham's Neeld Hall on September 30 1947, the auction was conducted by Knight, Frank and Rutley and was attended by a packed crowd of 200 people. The auction lasted three hours but failed to find a buyer for the village and manor house and so they were sold as individual lots, realising just over £39,000. This finally broke up the estate and ended the Barony after 850 years. Most of the land, including Upper Combe and the airfield, was retained by the estate in trust.

Significant in the move to get motorsport going again after the war was the Bristol Motor Cycle and Light Car Club, later simply to become the Bristol Motor Club. The local club can lay claim to running the first recognised event after the war when, as early as August 1945, it ran the Naish Hillclimb. This was an 800-yard grass and bare earth hill at Naish Hill House near Bristol for both cars and motorbikes. The fastest time of the day went to Peter Falconer on a 500cc Triumph while the car entry included Bob Gerard's ERA and Dennis Poore in an MG.

In 1948 and 1949, the club ran Speed Trials on Marine Parade at Weston Super Mare and in April 1949 ran its first race meeting on a two-mile circuit on the then disused Lulsgate airfield. That event was repeated in April 1950, but negotiations had already started with Kitty Maurice about using the disused Castle Combe airfield.

Chapter 2

The opening of the circuit

The impetus for creating a circuit at Castle Combe came from the Bristol MC & LCC's problems gaining RAC approval for further events at Lulsgate. Although race meetings were run at the Bristol venue in both 1949 and 1950, the club was well aware that another venue was urgently needed.

In the club's journal of February 1950, secretary Laurie Atkinson explained the position. 'We are having another fight with the RAC - quite friendly - to obtain a permit to use Lulsgate Bottom Aerodrome again for a sports car race meeting on the Saturday after Easter. It is painfully obvious that, even if we get permission for this aerodrome this year, it will be really the last time. However, your committee has not been idle and arrangements are well in hand to use Castle Combe Aerodrome through the interest and generosity of the present owner, the land having reverted to agricultural purposes. There are no runways but quite an interesting perimeter track, but a lot of work and some money will be required to make it suitable for racing. I am sure that, in the coming summer months, we can count on club members coming forward in large numbers to help in making this venue a permanent circuit for racing in the West of England. It is hoped that we may be able to organise a small meeting there sometime this year just to give the place a tryout ready for a much bigger event to replace Lulsgate next year.'

Chris Bigwood, a member and official of the Bristol club from the early 1950s recalled: 'Lulsgate wasn't very satisfactory, the RAC wasn't at all happy with it as a circuit. The people on the committee were mostly well known Bristol businessmen. A chap called Tom Simmonds was friendly with Mrs Kitty Maurice and he really set the whole thing up.' Simmonds was a builder who lived in Marshfield, not far from Castle Combe. Even before the first race was held, the club had long term ambitions for the new venue. 'It is the club's intention, as a long term policy, to make the fencing and facilities complete and permanent as funds permit,' said Atkinson in March 1950.

Progress was encouraging, and Atkinson's report a month later offered more information. 'RAC inspection should have been completed by now, thus allowing the club to proceed with all the work that will be required in the way of fencing, clearance of the track and road repairs. The aerodrome is now private property and is being farmed, and will only be open on race days; at other times there are fences across the track to keep the cattle in. Do not go out there on spec to try out your car, as you won't be able to get round the track,' he warned.

That was a warning that didn't reach Geoff Williams of the Wessex Centre of the Auto Cycle Union. Before the ACU began running motorcycle meetings at Castle Combe they went there to try out the track, probably in 1951. Williams was fortunate to escape major injury when he was pulled off his Vincent by a length of wire that the farmer had strung across the track.

In May, Atkinson reported latest developments. 'We have just received permission, from the solicitors of Mrs Maurice, the owner of Castle Combe Aerodrome, to proceed with our first meeting there on July 8th. It will

7

be quite a small meeting open to club members only but before this takes place quite a lot of the fencing will have to be altered and some new fences erected. The great beauty of this circuit from our point of view is that we shall be able to put up permanent fences which will not have to be hurriedly pulled down after each meeting. Mrs Maurice is very keen for this club to organise races at Castle Combe and is very kindly going out of her way to assist us in every direction. At the present moment her solicitors are drawing up an agreement which will give us racing rights on the circuit rent-free for two years whilst we get things organised. The club's general policy is to pay our way and gradually effect the necessary alterations and additions necessary to the circuit as and when we make sufficient money from the events we hope to run there. The RAC Competitions Department, in the person of Mr. Dean Delamont, has already inspected the course.'

'A lot of work to get the circuit ready was done by the members who would turn out and work really hard. Even though they were businessmen they got their sleeves rolled up and got on with it,' says Bigwood.

'There were many remnants from RAF days including a pill box that we literally had to blow up to get rid of, which was great fun. There was also a haystack in the middle of the main straight and lots of clearing up to do behind the herd of cows which had been grazing there,' remembered Mike Edkins. Indeed, this would be a problem throughout the early years as a herd of cows crossed the circuit on Farm Straight twice a day for milking. Other work included breaking up old concrete paths in the Old Paddock area and Gerry Millington of the club recalls spending time in a mechanical digger breaking up concrete to make the run-off safer.

By June, negotiations were being completed and the first meeting would be able to go ahead as planned. In his June report, Atkinson commented: 'The arrangements regarding Castle Combe are making very good progress and a draft agreement has been drawn up between the club, Mrs Maurice (the landowner) and the farmer who rents the land and should be ratified shortly. We have it on good authority that Development Charges will not be levied on our use of the land, provided that we do not use the circuit for more than 28 days in the year. Written

confirmation from the Land Development Board is awaited on this point before arrangements are finally settled. It is the club's intention to use Castle Combe to provide racing for the club member who has a sports car or motorcycle, rather than to stage regular racing spectacles with well-known drivers taking part. We shall possibly hold one open meeting a year there.'

'The first meeting was effectively a private meeting. You were not allowed to have the public in the first time you ran an organised race meeting. That was in July 1950 and in October they ran a public meeting,' says Strawford. Sure enough, on July 8th the Bristol club ran a successful inaugural meeting at Castle Combe.

The programme for that first meeting noted: 'Before any meeting open to the general public can be staged, much time and money will have to be expended on permanent fencing to comply with the requirements of the RAC regarding the safety and control of spectators. We intend to complete sufficient of this fencing to enable us to hold a National Race Meeting here on October 7th.'

Far from being just the landowner, Mrs Maurice took a very active involvement in race meetings. 'She encouraged them to run bigger meetings. So much so, that she became secretary of the meetings for the Bristol club and amazing though it may seem, she used to travel around the race tracks of Europe, trying to persuade teams to come along and race,' says Strawford.

The main officials for that very first meeting included Tom Simmonds (Clerk of the Course), Eric Storey (Chief Marshal), Russell Ashby (Starter), Jack Ashby (Judge), Tony Hemmens (Timekeeper) and Cliff Salter (Secretary of the Meeting). Russell Ashby was the starter at Prescott hillclimb both before and after the war and had been the winning navigator on the 1937 RAC Rally. Commentators were Wilf Kay and Pat McCormick, but Wilf split his time between talking and racing a 4-litre supercharged Allard. The event programme also noted that a mechanical sweeper had kindly been loaned by British Quarrying Co. Ltd.

Eight races were arranged for July 8th, starting with a 10-lap race for Clubmans' motorbikes, followed by seven 5-lap car races. Four were for sportscars, one for saloons,

October 1950, the start of the 500cc F3 race.

Photo: Ferret Fotographics.

one for specials and one for 500cc Formula 3s. All competitors that day were presented with a cigarette lighter engraved with the event details and their name. The motorbikes had the honour of opening the racing history of Castle Combe and the field comprised four 500cc and three 350cc machines. DJP Wilkins (Triumph 500) entered by Archie Allen) led throughout to win but was chased hard by Franz Pados (350 Douglas), while Archie Allen (350 Douglas) and DM Gadd (500 Vincent) almost dead-heated for third place.

The second race was for sports cars up to 1100cc or 850cc supercharged and was won by Jim Sparrowe in an 1100cc Morgan at an average speed of 62.5mph. Second was Arthur Mallock, who would later go on to gain fame and respect for his range of sports-racing cars that would still be winning races at the circuit 50 years later. Race three was another sports cars event, this time for cars 1101 - 1500cc or 851 - 1100cc supercharged. The winner

was Gerry Ruddock (HRG) with Jim Sparrowe second in his Morgan. Other notable entries included Ken Downing (Connaught), CDF Buckler (Buckler), John Buncombe (HRG) and Brian Owens (Frazer Nash).

Tony Crook powered his 1971cc Frazer Nash to back-to-back victories in the next pair of races, firstly for sports cars 1501 - 2000cc or 1101 - 1500cc supercharged and then in race five for sports cars over 2000cc or over 1500cc supercharged. Crook swapped to a Bristol 401 for the next event for saloon cars but was headed by Ken Downing in a Healey. Although always an amateur racer, Downing would go on to compete in two grands prix before retiring from the sport in 1953.

The seventh race was for specials, cars that had never been taxed or insured on public highways. It was won by John Bendle in his MG-based special while the final race of the day was for 500cc racing cars to international

Formula 3 regulations. It was won by Clive Lones (Iota Tiger Kitten II) at an average of 66.5 mph from Gerry Millington (Milliunion) and Vic Worlock (Worlock). Also on the entry list was joint commentator Pat McCormick (McCormick).

Although the races were timed, it seems probable that no individual lap times were taken although the honour of the first Castle Combe outright circuit record almost certainly fell to Tony Crook who lapped his Frazer Nash at an average speed of 75mph. What is certain is that the first meeting had been a great success and the Bristol club pressed ahead with plans for the next meeting on October 7th 1950, which would open Castle Combe to the public for the first time.

conditions in its gentle undulations and succession of bends and corners.

The Autocar report of the time commented on the challenge offered by Quarry Corner. 'This is the main hazard, preceded by a bend to the left and a series of bumps, and it goes a long way towards making the course interesting. Spectators are well catered for and can get a good view of two corners, including Quarry, and the start-finish line. The paddock is on a concrete area on the far side of the course from the spectators.'

Public interest ran high for there were few race circuits operating in Britain at the time. Lulsgate had hosted its second and final meeting in April and the

October 1950, the formation lap for the F3 race.

The race programme noted names for the major corners as Camp, Quarry, and Tower while the straight after Quarry was called Farm Straight. The paddock area was located on the far side of circuit from the start/finish line, adjacent to the corner that became known as Old Paddock. At the time, this was a sizeable concrete area where hangars had been built. The programme described the circuit as approximately 1.9 miles in length and 35 to 50 ft in width, presenting a near approach to true road

fledgling Brands Hatch was just opening. Blandford Camp, Gamston and Winfield would be closed to racing by the end of 1951. Goodwood and Silverstone had both hosted first meetings in 1948 and Croft held racing for seven years from 1950 before closing for seven years. From 1950, only Silverstone, Brands Hatch and Castle Combe have a continuous motorsport history amongst British circuits.

The second F3 heat on October 7th, 1950. Stirling Moss lies in second place behind A. Rogers.

stiff breeze dried the track in time for most of the racing, which opened with the pair of Formula 3 heats.

The first heat produced an easy win by Ronald 'Curly' Dryden in a Cooper-Norton. Dryden was one of the leading Formula 3 drivers of the time, nicknamed Curly as he was completely devoid of hair. The second heat featured a chaotic start as several cars stalled. But once underway, there was a tremendous dice between the Cooper-Nortons of Peter Collins and Stirling Moss as they traded the lead many times. Ultimately, Moss won after Collins was delayed lapping backmarkers. Both, would, of course, go on to become world-famous racers.

Having successfully run seven races in July, the club extended the programme to nine races in October, including two heats for Formula 3 cars. Spectators were charged 5 shillings, with 5 shillings for car parking, which was outside the circuit. Spectators were allowed all round the circuit except for the section along Farm Straight. Local newspapers estimated the crowd at 12,000.

With the paddock area on the far side of circuit from the start/finish line, cars had half a lap in which to warm-up before the start. Practice was untimed and grid positions were decided by ballot, apart from the 500 race which was by heat results, with pole position on the left of grid. No less than six cars were lined up on the front row of the grid. Drivers were recommended to wear crash helmets, but it was not mandatory. Corner marking flags were supplied by the Avon India Rubber Co and corner indicators by Newton Oils.

Spectators were scantily protected by rope barriers and straw bales. 'The safety element for the public was negligible. People didn't use to worry much in those days,' said Russell Ashby. A total of £275 in prize money was on offer and the meeting attracted a very healthy entry of around 110. Despite rain during the morning, a

Later in the afternoon was the eagerly-awaited Formula 3 final. However, hopes for a repeat of the Moss/Collins battle were dashed when Moss made a terrible start and was well down the field on the opening lap. At the head of the field, Dryden and Collins were battling hard as Moss set about recovering lost ground. He made up eight places in a single lap before slowing with engine problems. The Collins/Dryden battle continued with Collins winning by a couple of lengths from Dryden, and Ian Burgess took third.

Ken Wharton won race three for racing cars from 500 - 1000cc in a Cooper JAP while more of the star names of the era were out for race four for racing cars from 1100 - 1500cc. Collins (Cooper-JAP 1200) made a superb start to lead the ERAs into Quarry, but power soon told and Collins was passed by Bob Gerard (R14B) and Brian Shawe Taylor (R9B) on Farm Straight. Gerard won from Shawe-Taylor with Collins fending off Graham Whitehead (R10B) for third.

October 1950. The F3 field lines up including Ken Gregory (31) and Peter Collins (24).

Ken Wharton (ERA) led until hit by gearbox problems.

Moss made up for his Formula 3 problems by winning race five for racing cars 1500-2500cc. His victory followed a titanic struggle between Wharton in Peter Bell's 2-litre ERA (R11B) and Moss in a 2-litre HWM. Wharton retired the ERA with gearbox trouble with a couple of laps to go, leaving Moss to win comfortably from Ken McAlpine, who was giving the new F2 Connaught its debut.

After the excitement of the racing car action, two sports car races were next up. In the up to 2-litre race, Moss (in David Murray's Frazer Nash Le Mans) and Crook (Frazer Nash) battled for the lead before Moss went ahead to take his third win of the day. Also competing was John Cooper in a 1250cc MGTC-engined Cooper fitted with cycle-type wings and Joan Gerard, wife of Bob, in a Frazer Nash Le Mans. In the race for over 2-litre sports cars, Sydney Allard (5.4 Allard J2

Cadillac) ran away with the race and came close to lapping the entire field.

The final race of a busy afternoon was for Formula Libre and was won comfortably by Shawe-Taylor (ERA) from Whitehead (ERA) and Moss (F2 HWM). Shawe-Taylor took the honour of the first recorded outright circuit record with a lap in 1m20.2s, an average speed of 82.6mph to bring the meeting to a fitting conclusion.

There is no doubt that the first public meeting was a huge success. The Bristol MC & LCC journal of the period reports driver reaction to the new circuit. 'Stirling Moss says the best way of describing the course is that it is of a very sporting nature: doesn't mind the bumps much, but when told of the RAC's invitation to run an international said that the whole circuit would need to be resurfaced for such an event. Tony Crook was here in July when we couldn't see the corners for grass and says the grass cutting is a decided improvement.'

However, the first warning shots were also fired in what would become an ever-present battle for the fledgling circuit. The Wiltshire Gazette chose only to list the results and not carry a report on the meeting other than running a very negative reaction. 'For the second time this year the peace and quiet of the Castle Combe countryside was shattered by the searing screech of supercharged racing engines on Saturday, when the Bristol MC&LCC held its first public race meeting for cars at the aerodrome circuit.'

However, adverse reaction from some of the local media was not a major concern to the club at the time and preparations went ahead for the 1951 season. Key amongst the planned changes was the re-siting of the paddock to the northern end of the circuit. The re-location of the paddock also brought about a corner name change as the original Paddock Corner was re-named Old Paddock. Kitty Maurice spent some time chasing the local Council to obtain Ministry of Health sanction for the de-requisitioning of this land to improve facilities for both competitors and spectators.

Reports in the Bristol club's journal of March 1951 also noted the fencing work that was planned. 'After voting a considerable sum of money towards it (£200),

the work of fencing at Castle Combe was started at the beginning of February. This will consist of fencing in the paddock area which is now at the north end of the circuit on the hard standing adjacent to the main entrance, and blocking up with high fences those large gaps in the hedge surrounding the field through which so many spectators came in for nothing at the last meeting.'

The date for the first meeting of 1951 was set for March 31st, but a great deal of work was needed to get the track ready. Once again, everything relied on willing volunteers. 'The few who did turn up for working parties had to erect about one mile of rope and stake fencing, some three hundred stakes to drive in, the whole of the course had to be swept, particularly Quarry Corner which had been used for feeding cows. It was like a stable! There was the dummy and starting grid and all the paddock numbers to be painted, straw bales to be placed at corners, corner markers to set out, pay boxes to erect and a host of other jobs,' said Laurie Atkinson at the time.

Before that first race meeting, plans had been made to run a members' practice day on February 12. 'The first arrivals at the circuit were horrified to find that the farmer had apparently been bedding and feeding his beasts all winter on the whole of the track between Quarry Corner and Paddock Bend. The surface would have been a credit to any trials organiser, consisting as it did of about three inches of rich top dressing bound together with odd lengths of bailing wire. However the mechanical sweeper started work and, helped by allcomers, cleared the track to such good effect that the only comments received were on the fruity taste of the spray in that section,' said Gerald Husband of the Bristol club. Sleet and snow added to the challenge of the day.

'In the early days everything had to be taken to the circuit for the meeting, nothing was kept there. We were able to use lorries from club members' businesses. Preparation was hard graft for a couple of weeks for relatively few people. There was tremendous club spirit,' recalls Chris Bigwood. A further members' practice meeting had been held on April 28 for both cars and motorcycles. However, before that, the first public meeting of 1951 had been held on March 31 and had spotlighted a fine young talent. Mike Hawthorn would go on to become Britain's first world champion, but in 1951,

Mike Hawthorn and his
Riley in May 1951.

Photo: Geoff Williams.

John Hogan (BSA Bantam) during the
first dedicated motor cycle meeting in
July 1951.

Photo:
Mortons Motorcycle Media.

May 12, 1951. Hawthorn (far left) and Tony Crook (far right) head the field.

he was just a young hopeful with a Riley. It seems, however, that Hawthorn had tried to compete in the October 1950 meeting. But the Bristol club committee, when deciding who the reserves would be, consigned the unknown Hawthorn to the reserve list.

Hawthorn's sparkling form that afternoon netted two race wins and helped counter the cold, wet day. His first win came in the 1100cc sportscar race when he took his Riley 9 Ulster Imp to victory by over a minute from L Gibbs (Riley 9) and Jim Sparrowe (Morgan). In race three, for 1500cc sportscars, he won in a 1.5-litre Riley and the Autosport report of the day recorded his pace: 'Hawthorn tore away from his rivals and, despite a couple of excursions into the rough, was unchallenged for the entire distance.' This was only Hawthorn's second ever race meeting, the first being at Gamston five days earlier.

Other winners that day included Don Parker and Ken Carter in the Formula 3 heats, Dickie Stoop (Mille Miglia Frazer-Nash), Oscar Moore (HWM) and John Bolster who raced a 1911 Rolls-Royce Silver Ghost with considerable verve to win a 5-lap handicap for Veteran & Edwardian cars. However, it was the Formula 3 final that was the highlight of the day with 20 cars battling over 10 laps.

Parker led from the start with Bill Whitehouse, (Cooper Norton), Clive Lones (Iota Tiger Kitten), Ken Wharton (Cooper Norton) and Les Leston (JBS-JAP) in pursuit. Then Lones had a big spin at Quarry, losing half a dozen places in the process and lucky to avoid being hit by the following cars. Parker and Wharton battled for the lead until Parker spun into Quarry and was hit by Wharton. That put Parker out with a damaged wheel but Wharton was able to continue despite riding up over Parker's wheel. The chasing pack of five cars all took to the grass but they all continued, with Whitehouse now ahead. However, Wharton was not about to give in and battled back to win by two seconds from Carter and Jack Moor (Wasp-Norton). Peter Collins had also been racing but his engine seized early in the race.

The programme included four motorcycle races and the general public were not admitted. Bristol club members were admitted to the circuit by ticket only. Hawthorn again won twice while another victory went to

Colin Chapman in his Lotus Mk3. This was the debut race for the Mk3 Lotus, the first Lotus designed purely for circuit racing. In practice, Chapman had a problem when drops of fuel blew into his face at high speed. But this was fixed for the race by fitting a forward facing air intake made from radiator hose. Winners of the motorcycle races were JR Hill (350 BSA), BJ Thompson (350 AJS) and WG Baxter (350 Triumph) who won twice. Baxter also set the fastest motorbike lap of the day in 74.9mph which probably represents the first official motorbike outright circuit lap record.

The circuit's first dedicated motorcycle meeting was held on July 28 and was organised by the Bristol club with invitations to the Wessex Centre ACU clubs. Highlights of the day were the sidecar race and a thrilling 500cc final. After eight hard-fought laps, the sidecar race was won by Pip Harris (600 Norton) from C Smith (500 Norton) and Bill Boddice (500 Norton), the trio being covered by a scant fifth of a second at the finish. The 15-lap 500cc final featured a race-long battle between HL Williams (500 Norton) and PES Webb (500 JABS), with Williams winning by a bike's length and setting a new record at an average of 79.04mph.

However, while the circuit's reputation grew, all was not rosy on the organisational front. The Bristol club's accounts for the period 6 April to 30 September 1951 show losses on Castle Combe events of over £156, with a substantial loss on the motor-cycle meeting. Additionally, expenditure on Castle Combe repairs of £174 led to a financial crisis in July. The problem was resolved, for the time being at least, by devising a scheme of loans from members. The final meeting of the season, a national car race meeting, improved finances somewhat.

On October 6, between 10,000 and 15,000 spectators packed the circuit to see Wharton and Gerard take the major races in ERAs and Gerard take the circuit record below 1m20s for the first time. His best lap of 1m19.2s (83.64mph) would be the standard for just 12 months until he came back and comprehensively lowered the record. Tragically, the meeting also produced the first fatal accident at the circuit when Curley Dryden was killed in the Formula 3 race.

The tragedy struck in the second Formula 3 heat. Don Parker had beaten Ken Wharton in the first heat but the meeting was marred when Dryden crashed at Camp on the first lap while leading. His JBS slid wide and overturned, inflicting fatal head injuries to the popular and successful racer. Les Leston won the heat while Charles Headland (Kieft-Norton) led the final from start to finish. Bob Gerard (Cooper-Norton) started nearly last but climbed through the field to finish second, less than half a second behind Headland. To complete a black day, John Habin (JBS) rolled at Old Paddock and was hospitalised with a broken jaw.

The paddock in October 1951.

Photo: Brian Owens.

Sidney Allard (5.4 Allard Cadillac), Ken Wharton (Peter Bell ERA), Cliff Davis (Cooper-MG) and George Abecassis (HWM) all took victories, Abecassis having an easy time in the 1500 - 2500cc racing car event after Duncan Hamilton's HWM blew its engine in practice.

Mike Hawthorn in his Riley.

Photo: LAT

The solid silver Hastings Trophy was awarded to Gerard for winning the Formula Libre race, but it was Wharton who suffered the most drama. According to the Autosport report of the race: 'On lap four, as the ERA came into Paddock Bend a veritable fireworks display appeared beneath it, the back wheels locked and it slid onto the grass. Ken jumped out (hurriedly) and beat at the legs of his overalls. He then attacked the fire with the seat cushion until fire extinguishers were brought across the track. The universal joint behind the Wilson gearbox had seized setting alight the electron casing.'

And so the second season of Castle Combe came to a conclusion. But the Bristol club was already laying plans for an increased programme for 1952.

Chapter 3

World Champions
and
Formula One races

The successful October 1951 meeting had given the Bristol club's finances a much-needed boost and so plans were made for 1952. New in the paddock was a footbridge over the paddock exit road, constructed with the support of Avon Tyres. Four meetings, including one for motorbikes were confirmed and temporary planning permission was obtained. It was the start of all the planning battles that would dog the circuit's history, and yet a simple form and tiny fee back then could have made so much difference.

'When the Town and Country Planning Act was introduced in 1952, the circuit operators applied for planning permission and were granted temporary planning permission, to decide various levels and conditions of usage. Badly advised, this was allowed to run on for over 10 years. In fact a Certificate of Established Usage could have been originally obtained for the sum of five shillings,' says Howard Strawford.

No one was aware of the significance of all this, of course, when the 1952 season kicked off with a meeting on Easter Saturday. This had originally been planned as an international 500cc meeting but sponsorship was not found and facing a predicted loss of around £200, the club decided to run closed invitation races instead. Grid positions for all races were decided by ballot and the meeting was headlined by Stirling Moss winning the F3 race and Castle Combe regular Tony Crook taking two wins in entertaining sports car races.

Moss won his Formula 3 heat but that was little consolation when he drew the back row of the grid for the final in the ballot. Despite that considerable handicap, Stirling showed his class by going on to win the 10-lap final at a canter in his Kieft. The other two heats were won by Michael Barclay (Cooper JAP) and Don Truman (Cooper Norton).

Tony Crook and Roy Salvadori (Frazer Nash Le Mans Replica) dominated the 2500cc sportscar race and played to the gallery by changing places constantly before Crook won by half a length. 'There was no real opposition and we were able to play around,' recalled Salvadori. Both cars were prepared by Crook, who had to work considerably harder in the race for unlimited sports cars.

Apart from Salvadori, the opposition included the Ecurie Ecosse Jaguar XK120s of Ian Stewart, Bill Dobson and Sir James Scott-Douglas. The long haul to Wiltshire represented only the second race meeting for the newly formed Ecurie Ecosse, and was its first foray out of Scotland. Scott-Douglas led from the start but a determined Crook powered ahead at Old Paddock and held on for a famous win as Stewart and Salvadori chased him home. Motor Sport magazine noted the fledgling Ecurie Ecosse team: 'The management and pit-work of this Ecurie are noteworthy and they should go far.'

After an hour's break for tea when timekeepers worked out handicaps and corners were swept, the final race was a handicap relay race covering nine laps for teams of three cars. It was won by John Buncombe (Healey Silverstone), MRC Llewellyn (MG TD), and JK

April 1952, the Ecurie Ecosse Jaguar XK120s in the paddock.

Photo: Ferret Fotographics.

John Buncombe's Healey in April 1952.

Photo: Ferret Fotographics.

Hemsworth (Jaguar XK120), with the Ecurie Ecosse Jaguars third. The Motor report recorded the light-hearted nature of the race. 'The last race of the day was a handicap relay, which was very complicated but great fun. Crook did an extra lap by mistake, thus disqualifying his team, of which the other members were Moss and Salvadori. So enraged were those gentlemen that they set about the unhappy Crook with their crash-hats; it was just as well that he was still wearing his.'

Repeating the successful meeting of 12 months earlier, the May meeting was closed to the Bristol and 750 clubs and was a combined car and motorcycle meeting. Unfortunately, it was held in almost continuous rain. Major winners were Les Leston (Formula 3) and Oscar Moore (HWM-Jaguar) in the Formula Libre race while Geoff Tapp took a pair of wins in his Buckler. 750MC member Douglas Cross was trying to repair a magneto for a competitor and recalled the conditions that day. 'I begged space and dryness from the paddock marshal and tools from everyone. We finished up in an air-raid shelter, in which some enterprising types had built a fire to dry out their underwear.'

On September 6 the circuit hosted its first national motorcycle meeting, which was jointly organised by the ACU Wessex Centre and the Bristol club. Nine races attracted over 150 riders and an estimated 8,000 crowd. Having taken a significant financial loss on the corresponding meeting in 1951, the arrangements were changed for 1952. 'It will be run jointly with the Wessex Centre ACU under a generous and one-sided agreement whereby we share the profits 50/50 but the Wessex Centre stand any loss,' reported the Bristol club Journal in June. By agreeing to underwrite the meeting, the ACU proved just how keen the motorcycle racing fraternity was to have Castle Combe on its calendar.

The Junior 350 final was a thriller and was won by BWT Rood (AJS). However, the star of the day was John Surtees who won both his heat and the final of the 500cc race on his Norton. In the process, he took the motorcycle lap record past the 80mph mark for the first time and set a standard that would stand for two seasons before he went faster still. Reporting on the meeting, Motor Cycle magazine described the circuit: 'The 1.84-

mile circuit, with its natural undulations, is rather nearer a road circuit than most airfield perimeters.'

The now traditional early October national meeting concluded the programme on Saturday October 3, but for the first time featured practice on Friday. Also new was a temporary grandstand opposite the pits. Records of that meeting show a crowd of 10,719 and 7500 programmes sold with just under 2000 cars in the car parks. The meeting netted a profit of just over £400. Notable winners were Roy Salvadori (Ferrari) in the Fry Memorial Trophy Formula 2 race, Bob Gerard (ERA) in the Hastings Trophy Formula Libre race and Stirling Moss in the Formula 3 race.

In the Formula 3 final Moss led Don Parker throughout, as Les Leston (Leston-Norton) finished third and Stuart Lewis-Evans (Cooper) fourth. Moss set a new Formula 3 record at an average speed of 80.59mph while Ken Tyrrell (Cooper) went grass mowing at Old Paddock according to race reports.

In the up to 1500cc sportscar race Gillie Tyrer (Fiat-engined BMW special) led throughout winning from Cliff Davies (Cooper MG). According to period reports, this race included the first appearance of a Porsche in a British race when CL Bannister raced a left-hooker 356. The Ecurie Ecosse team returned for the over 1500cc sportscar race and made up for being beaten by Tony Crook at Easter when Ian Stewart took a commanding victory, this time at the wheel of a glorious C Type Jaguar. He also set the first sportscar lap at more than 80mph.

In practice for the Fry Memorial Trophy Formula 2 race Stirling Moss lapped beneath the outright course record in practice in a G-Type ERA. The race was broken up by a three-car incident on the opening lap at Old Paddock when Barber's Cooper-Bristol spun and collided first with Brown's Cooper-Bristol and then with Whitehead's Alta. All three cars were too badly damaged to continue. The lead was contested for the first six laps by Moss and Roy Salvadori in Bobbie Baird's Ferrari Tipo 500 F2. But Moss retired on lap seven, leaving Salvadori with a commanding lead. Ken Wharton (Cooper-Bristol) was second from the similar Ecurie

David Blakeley's HRG in 1953. Ruth Ellis would later be hung for his murder.

Photo: Ferret Fotographics.

Ecosse entered car of Ninian Sanderson. Salvadori set a new circuit lap record at an average of 85.38mph but it would stand only fleetingly and was broken again before the end of the afternoon. The Fry Trophy was a specially commissioned model from professional model maker Harold Pratley of Joe Fry's famous Freikaiserwagen. Fry, a member of the Fry's chocolate family and a Bristol club member, had been killed at Blandford in 1950 when racing his unique special.

The Hastings Trophy Formula Libre race ran over 15 laps and brought the curtain down on the 1952 season as Bob Gerard (2-litre ERA) led from start to finish, ten seconds clear of Peter Walker (Cooper ERA). Walker's rare car was a lengthened Cooper Bristol chassis to take the 6-cylinder supercharged ERA engine. Gerard also showed his mastery of Castle Combe by setting a new lap record of 1m16.8s, (86.25mph), nearly two and a half seconds faster than his own 1951 standard.

Finally, the October meeting included a demonstration run by John Cooper in an aerodynamic record breaking Cooper. This featured an all-enveloping body on a Mk V Cooper-Norton in which John won the first 500 F3 race run at an average of more than 100mph on August 31 at Grenzlandring in Germany. Other stories from that meeting included the fact that F3 racer Paul Emery and his team spent Friday night in the timing bus having been let down over hotel accommodation. Listed in the programme was Tony Brooks in a Healey, but there is no confirmation of him actually racing.

The 1953 season opened, as the previous year, with a meeting on Easter Saturday, April 4. For the first time, spectators were permitted to park their cars close to the edge of the circuit. Highlight of the day, which ended in a hailstorm, was Dennis Taylor winning the Formula 3 race in the new Martin Special after Don Parker was delayed by a backmarker at Quarry on the last lap. Also among the Formula 3 field was Ivor Bueb from Cheltenham in an Arnott. He would go on to win Le Mans twice for Jaguar before, but at Castle Combe in 1953 he was simply one of the rising stars of Formula 3. Oscar Moore (HWM Jaguar) and Cliff Davis (Cooper MG) were other winners during a relatively uneventful meeting.

Three weeks later the circuit was back in use for the Bristol/750MC meeting which again included four motorcycle races. Headline race was for Formula 3 cars and it was Bournemouth-domiciled Belgian Andre Loens (Kieft) who fended off Les Leston for victory. Motorcycle races were won by RA Ingram (500 Matchless), CM Luck (350 Velocette), LW Taylor (500 Norton Sidecar) and E Pantlin (490 Norton).

Surtees starred at the July national motorcycle meeting which drew an impressive 10,000 spectators. He easily won the junior and senior races on a pair of Nortons and set a new junior record at 80mph. Any hopes that he would top the circuit record during the 500 event were thwarted by rain. The meeting was run solely by the Wessex Centre of the ACU and that was an arrangement that would continue for nearly 20 years. Comprising around 20 motorcycle clubs from Bristol, north and west Wiltshire and north Somerset, the Wessex Centre drew organisers and marshals from all member clubs. The leading figure in relation to Castle Combe was Vic Anstice, who was secretary of the meeting from 1952 until 1971, having previously been a works Douglas rider in TTs and Grands Prix in the 1920s.

With a three-month gap in the circuit calendar, the Bristol club took the opportunity to carry out some improvement before the national meeting on Saturday October 3. Most notable was that the approach to Quarry was resurfaced to reduce bumps. It was a cracking meeting and the crowd was estimated at 20,000. If correct, this represented the biggest crowd so far in the circuit's three-year history and was excellent news for the Bristol MC & LCC.

Ken Wharton, one of the sport's greatest all-rounders, won the Formula Libre race in his BRM V16 and smashed the circuit lap record, paring a massive three seconds from Bob Gerard's year-old mark. Incredibly,

Wharton's 1m13.8s lap was only a whisker shy of the 90mph average and represented a 15mph increase since the circuit's first meeting three and a half years earlier. As an indication of Wharton's speed that day, his average speed for the 15-lap Hastings Trophy race was higher than the previous lap record. He won by more than half a minute despite several car problems which included a failed right-hand front strut, low pressure in a right-hand rear tyre and a leaking radiator.

Bob Gerard (Cooper-Bristol) won the Formula 2 race and Reg Parnell (Aston Martin DB3S) won the sports car race. There was more drama when Stirling Moss fractured his shoulder after rolling in the Formula 2 race. Although he won his Formula 3 heat, Moss was forced to miss the final after his Formula 2 accident and that left the way open for Don Parker to beat Les Leston by a fraction of a second after a fine battle.

In the Fry Memorial Trophy Formula 2 race Moss had the most serious accident of his career at the time when his Cooper was clipped by the Connaught of Tony Rolt on the entry to Quarry on the second lap. The Cooper rolled and Moss was thrown out, and was perhaps fortunate to escape more serious injuries. Motor Sport reported his injuries as a broken knee-cap, broken collar bone, abrasions and shock. After a night in the Bristol Royal Infirmary, Moss was discharged. He later described the accident in detail. 'As I braked hard for Quarry Corner the Cooper slowed with its normal efficiency but that proved too much for the braking ability of Rob Walker's Connaught, which was right behind me driven by Tony Rolt. He was taken by surprise and was quite unable to avoid running into me, which sent the little Cooper somersaulting off the road. It threw me out on the way. I picked myself up and ran to safety before collapsing with a broken shoulder, damaged arm and twisted knee.' It took 12 weeks for the fractured shoulder to heal.

Gerard went on to win the race as the Cooper Bristols of Horace Gould and Wharton disputed second. The place narrowly went to Gould, a burly Bristolian garage owner, dubbed 'the Gonzales of the West Country' owing to his driving style mirroring that of Froilan Gonzales. A young mechanic with Gould at the time was Terry Sanger, who would later achieve considerable notoriety as a racer on two and four wheels.

'I was mechanic for Horace Gould on a few occasions and went to the Davidstow circuit in Cornwall with him the day he knocked the bridge down. I went to Castle Combe several times with him,' recalls Sanger. His own competition started in 1950 as a 16 year-old riding a BSA Gold Star and he would still be racing cars at the close of the 1999 season.

The October 1953 meeting was also notable for the fact that Kitty Maurice took on the role of Secretary of the Meeting for the first time, having already served as Vice-President and then Vice-Chairman of the club. It was a post she would hold for two years before standing down due to ill-health. 'Kitty was a character and a half. She was the only one I came across who could stand up to Horace Gould. His language was appalling and hers was worse. And yet she was one of the most cultivated people you could ever come across,' remembers Chris Bigwood.

The 1954 season started at Easter and the circuit was swamped as a bigger than ever crowd tried to get in. According to Autosport, there was traffic chaos. 'The main car park was full and auxiliary parks had to be organised for the huge crowd which blocked the roads leading to the circuit. Long after racing started strings of cars lay nose to tail on all adjacent roads.' The surge in spectator attendance seems to have been linked to the expected British debut of the new Maserati 250F. Roy Salvadori was entered to drive Sid Greene's new 250F, but the car failed to arrive from Italy in time. However, Maserati was still well represented as Salvadori took a brace of sportscar wins in Greene's 2-litre A6G.

Reg Bicknell was the man to beat in Formula 3 that day in his semi-streamlined Revis, winning both a heat and the final. However, many officials will remember the final for the narrow escape they had when Don Parker's Kieft had a very near miss with the timekeepers' bus.

Jimmy Stewart and Wilkie Wilkinson (sitting in car) with their C Type Jaguar in April 1954.
Photo: Ferret Fotographics.

Autosport reported the incident. 'As the field streamed out of Camp Corner, Parker, in second place, seemed to be taking a curious line. Officials in the infield scattered when it became obvious that something was seriously wrong. The Kieft came out of the bend, and made straight for the timekeepers' bus, narrowly missing a collision with a parked breakdown truck and crashing through a softwood barrier forming a small judges' enclosure. Parker was unhurt and said his steering locked solid and he could do nothing about it!'

Chris Bigwood also recalls the incident. 'The bus was on the inside of the circuit. We had a palisade around the front of the bus to create a sort of VIP area. I remember very well being in there when Don Parker came round and lost it at Camp Corner and came hurtling through this palisade, while I was holding a pint of beer in my hand, and he just went straight through it. Everybody just managed to get out of the way.'

The unlimited sports car race was memorable for a tremendous duel between Ecurie Ecosse's Jimmy Stewart (ex-works lightweight C-type Jaguar) and Salvadori (Maserati). Stewart took the lead and held it until the last lap when the Maserati got alongside at Old Paddock Bend. The Jaguar spun onto the grass and Stewart just managed to get back onto the circuit ahead of George Abecassis in his very rapid HWM.

Formula Libre victory went to Les Leston (1100cc Cooper-JAP) from Jimmy Stewart's Ecurie Ecosse Formula 2 Connaught which battled through the field after a poor start. Having narrowly missed disaster with Parker's Formula 3 car, a further incident in the day could have had equally dire consequences, as Motor Sport reported: 'On the last lap but one a very nasty incident involved JD Lewis (ERA). He went onto the grass after Quarry Corner and the ERA spun. It just missed a plough

The battered ERA of Lewis after its clash with a plough.
Photo: Ferret Fotographics.

standing on the edge of the course on the inside, just missed a head on crash into a second plough similarly placed, but caught this with its tail, which was badly crumpled. It continued as far as Old Paddock Bend with fuel gushing from the crumpled tank, until the engine stopped.'

John Surtees was back to dominate the July national motorcycle meeting, winning the 250, 350 Junior and Senior races. In the Senior race he broke his two-year-old lap record to leave the new mark at over 83mph on his 500 Norton. Maurice Cann (125 Mondial), Pip Harris (500 Norton sidecar), Max Klein (500 Norton sidecar handicap), CW Rous (500 AJS) and RE Gerard (350 Norton) also took wins, but it had been another display of the prodigious ability of Surtees.

Negotiations with the tenant farmer enabled spectator access all round the circuit for the 1954 national meeting, which was brought forward from October to August 28. A pedestrian corridor along Farm Straight allowed total spectator access and a reputed 20,000 crowd packed the circuit. For the first time, a spectator grandstand was erected at Quarry for the occasion. The meeting included a demonstration run by the three Bristol team cars celebrating recent one-two-three finishes at Le Mans and Rheims. This was the first time the cars had been on public show in Britain since their successes.

However, the major reason for the bumper attendance was the expected debut of a British Formula 1 car. The Western Daily Press was one of the papers to pick up on the story: 'Added excitement for today's Castle Combe race meeting will be the debut of the first British racing car to be made to the new Formula 1. It is a 3.5-litre unsupercharged Jaguar HWM entered for the Formula Libre race. It will be driven by the Australian Tony Gage and has been entered by George Abecassis.'

'We gave the press the facts as we knew them, that the new car was coming to this meeting and was going to be quite interesting. What they developed from that was unbelievable and we had a crowd turn up many thousands more than usual and in the end it didn't come. We were nearly lynched by some people. It looked as if it was a set up job. One became very circumspect in what one said,' said Chris Bigwood, press officer for the Bristol club at the time.

Although Don Parker (Kieft) again won the Formula 3 race, Jim Russell set a new lap record at just over 83mph. A Junior 500 race was won by the Kieft of David Boshier-Jones and the ERA Anniversary Trophy race, which attracted only two starters, was won by Graham Whitehead. The unlimited sportscar race featured a long battle between Roy Salvadori (Maserati 2 litre) and the remarkable Archie Scott-Brown (Lister-Bristol), Salvadori won by less than half a second with Colin Chapman third in his Lotus Mk8.

Archie Scott-Brown (Lister Bristol) in August 1954.

Photo: Ferret Fotographics.

**Flockhart and the
BRM in the
paddock, August
1954.**

**Photo:
Ferret Fotographics.**

**Flockhart on his
way third in the
1954 Hastings
Trophy race.**

**Photo:
Ferret Fotographics.**

**Bob Gerard,
winner of the 1954
Hastings Trophy.**

**Photo:
Ferret Fotographics.**

The Fry Memorial Trophy Formula 1 race finally went to Horace Gould (Cooper Bristol) after first Reg Parnell (Ferrari 625) and then Bob Gerard (Cooper Bristol) stopped with mechanical dramas. Parnell suffered piston failure and Gerard was sidelined with broken steering. Having been denied the sight of the glorious Maserati 250F at the Easter meeting, Castle Combe fans were out of luck in August as well. The car had again been entered by Sid Greene for Salvadori but was stuck in British customs having been returned to Italy for repairs.

Having repaired his steering after the earlier problem, Gerard turned in a remarkable drive to battle ahead of both Gould and Ron Flockhart (BRM V16 MkII) to win the Hastings Trophy Formula Libre race by a slender margin from Flockhart. Neither approached Wharton's lap record of the previous year, but it was reported that Flockhart's BRM was suffering from brake problems and magneto trouble causing a misfire. Finally, the meeting also marked the first appearance of a Lotus fitted with a Coventry-Climax engine when Dick Steed raced his brand new MkVIII.

The 1954 season ended on a high, but the future of the circuit was not so clear. The finances of the Bristol club were still struggling while a massive motor racing disaster was just around the corner. The Le Mans disaster of 1955, when a car somersaulted into the crowd and claimed more than 80 lives, would forever re-define race circuit safety. Castle Combe would not escape the aftershocks of that dreadful accident in France.

Although the circuit still only hosted four or five race meetings each year, it was now being used at other times as well, as Tom Simmonds detailed in the Bristol club journal in May 1955: 'Our confidence in Castle Combe has not been in vain; the circuit is now in demand from various concerns for testing purposes from tyres to racing cars. Avon Tyres uses it exclusively for testing its tyres, both with motor cycles and cars. It was Avon who helped us with the erection of the footbridge over the track entrance, thus eliminating a bottleneck always experienced when the old crossing gates were used.' As well as locally-based Avon tyres, the Wiltshire police used the circuit for driver training and paid an annual fee of £30 for this facility.

However, all was far from bright for the circuit as the financial situation worsened, despite the size of the crowd at most meetings, as Simmonds explained: 'We are now in our sixth season. Our gates have been going from strength to strength. Our net profits have gone the other way and continued to shrink. Prize money and starting money make such very heavy inroads; the insidious and paralysing entertainment duty weaken the structure still further. Then comes the Rates. The balance at the end of the year is roughly halved by the Income Tax. We feel at every meeting that it may be our last, as we are about the only club having events of a national status without being sponsored.'

There is no question that the Bristol club was suffering major difficulties in trying to stage higher and higher profile meetings. Simmonds covered this concern: 'I always feel that Castle Combe will still run its couple of meetings a year. There is always the club spirit that a commercial concern does not have.'

Despite these pressing financial concerns, development of the facilities continued as the 1955 season started. 'Work is afoot for new commentators' accommodation on top of the control bus and a permanent second commentators' box on Old Paddock. The ex-RAF Control Tower is now available to members and guests on race days and provides a good view, good accommodation and good refreshments,' reported Simmonds.

The 1955 season opened on April 9 with Dan Margulies winning the 30-lap sports car race in his ex-Ecurie Ecosse Jaguar C-Type. That race also marked an appearance by Graham Hill who spent much of that season touring Europe as a travelling mechanic for Margulies. But before they set off on their tour, Hill got to race the car for the first time at Castle Combe that day in April. It was probably only his third ever car race and he diced for fifth in the Formula Libre race with Michael Burn (RGS Atalanta) before spinning down the order. Race winner was John Riseley-Pritchard (F2 Connaught).

The Formula 3 race was up to the standard now expected of Castle Combe and it was Don Parker (Kieft) who beat Dennis Taylor (Cooper Mk9) and Jim Russell

Ivor Bueb winning in October 1955.

(Cooper Mk9) by only six-tenths of a second. A Production Touring car race was led throughout by Angela Brown, daughter of Aston Martin founder David Brown, in a DB2/4.

The July 1955 motorcycle meeting was John Surtees' last appearance at Castle Combe and his final lap record of 84.94 mph would stand for another two years. He won the Junior 350 final on a Norton, the lightweight 250 race on a streamlined NSU Sportmax and the 20-lap Senior 500 race on a Norton. The following year he joined the MV Augusta team and scored the first of his seven World Championship titles. The meeting was held in fine, sunny weather but was marred by the death of Eric Shepherd (Triumph) who crashed at Tower and died in hospital shortly afterwards.

The third and final event of 1955 was to be one of the most ambitious ever staged at the Wiltshire track and was titled the International Empire News Meeting. The meeting moved back to its more traditional early October date and was headlined by the Avon Trophy Formula 1 race, which would run over 55 laps, a distance of 101 miles on October 1. It seems likely that this remains the longest car race ever run at the circuit.

The whole event was a bold gamble by the Bristol club as the desire to attract an international line-up for the non-championship Formula 1 race took the club to a new level of commercial activity. Considerable sums of starting money would need to be paid out to leading entrants and outside support for the meeting was going to be essential. The club's August journal gave more details. 'For the first time support from outside sources is being given to help a particular meeting. The Empire News, a Kemsley Sunday newspaper has promised a trophy for the free formula race and has undertaken to design, print and very largely distribute a comprehensive range of publicity material. Avon India Rubber Co and Redex are providing trophies and cash awards for the Formula 1 and unlimited sports car races.'

Earlier, the club had appealed to members for support. In May, the chairman of the Castle Combe committee wrote seeking loans to provide: 'Buffer capital which might be required to ensure a high grade entry - and for this purpose only would the amount loaned be used. Approximately £1,000 is required. So far we have been reasonably successful in our negotiations with entrants, but it cannot yet be said that we are out of the woods if a representative entry is to be ensured.'

Chris Bigwood recalls the situation clearly. 'Starting money was the biggest problem we had. It was a tremendous outlay for international drivers. We had to limit it, it was difficult to spread the budget over a few drivers, we could have had a lot of people if we could have afforded it.' Kitty Maurice was a key negotiator in this process and travelled extensively around Europe in her attempts to attract a world class entry. The prize fund offered totalled £620.

Despite the funding problems, the event drew live BBC radio coverage. A temporary 600-seat grandstand was built opposite the pits and a new row of pits was constructed on the inside of the circuit opposite the paddock. The track lined with 2,000 straw bales. Scrutineering and practice was held on the Friday before the event starting at 11am and the first race was at 11am on Saturday, which thankfully dawned dry and sunny. The Evening Post reported that 18,000 paying spectators were needed for the club to break even, but the Motor Sport report of the meeting suggested a small attendance. General admission 12s 6d with grandstand seats 30s.

The opening race was for Formula 3 cars and ran over a marathon 25 laps. Colin Davis set a new F3 record at 84.71mph, but then suffered driveshaft failure at Quarry on the 12th lap. The wheel flew off and struck a girl spectator, Diana Stokes, and she was taken to hospital with concussion. Jim Russell spun away a narrow lead at Camp just after half distance, leaving team mate Ivor Bueb to win from David Boshier-Jones and Keith Hall as Coopers filled the top three places. Russell made amends

in a later Formula 3 race, winning from Bueb and Davis whose car had been repaired.

The 2000cc sportscars competed for the Two Litre Trophy presented by the Bristol Aeroplane Company's Car Division. The 20-lap race featured a Le Mans-type start and Les Leston led from the start in Peter Bell's 1.5 litre Connaught. Ivor Bueb (works 1100cc Cooper-Climax Bobtail) moved up to second and then took over the lead and won when Leston slowed with engine problems. Bueb added his third win of the day in a later 2-litre sportscar race after Colin Chapman spun his Lotus Mk9 at Camp.

The big race of the day was the Avon Trophy Formula 1 race. Non-arrivals included Mike Hawthorn (Scuderia Ferrari Lancia D50). Chris Bigwood recalls turning down Hawthorn's entry: 'Ferrari wanted too much starting money and we said 'no', which was quite a novelty. They weren't used to that. £750 was a lot of money in those days.'

That left the way open for American Harry Schell (Vanwall) to lead from start to finish and set a new lap record at exactly 90mph, a lap time of 1m13.6s. Peter Walker pitted Rob Walker's Connaught B-type with suspected gearbox problems while Peter Collins (Owen Organisation Maserati 250F) went out with a broken De Dion tube before half-distance. Having hit trouble with the works BRM, Collins switched to the 250F but was forced to start from the back of grid, having not practised the Maserati. He was up to fourth by the end of lap one and passed Horace Gould for second on lap four before retiring. Louis Rosier retired his 250F with a broken shock absorber but Gould steered his similar car to second. Bob Gerard (Cooper Bristol) and Roy Salvadori battled hard for third with Gerard finally taking the place. He also won the Fry Memorial Trophy for first British driver in a British car.

The Redex International Trophy was held over 20 laps for unlimited sports cars and produced a real heart-breaker for Roy Salvadori (Aston Martin DB3S). He led easily and with a lap to go was 15 seconds ahead of George Abecassis (HWM-Jaguar) and Louis Rosier (Ferrari 750S). Then the Aston's transmission locked solid, leaving Abecassis to win by a fifth of a second from Rosier after they had battled side by side round Camp on the last lap. Noel Cunningham-Reid (HWM-Jaguar) was third from Mackay Fraser (Ferrari). Salvadori took the slim consolation of a new sports car record at an average speed of 85.58mph.

The Formula Libre race for the Empire News and Hastings Trophies allowed Schell his second win of the day in a second Vanwall. He won by 20 seconds after Ron Flockhart (BRM V16 MkII) led briefly. The entry for this race was similar to the Formula 1 race and marked the last works race appearance for the BRM V16.

Although the racing had been generally good, the meeting was far from a financial success and the Bristol club lost around £700 on the event. Overall, events at Castle Combe in 1955 showed a net loss of £267 while the club's other activities showed a profit of £186. Undeterred, at this point, the club officials met in early December to start planning the 1956 season, subject to satisfactory reports on the circuit from the RAC Inspection Committee in January.

'The Castle Combe committee is now busy formulating its plans for the first meeting of the 1956 season, which we hope to promote on April 7th. The meeting will be a closed invitation event with a vintage car handicap as well as races for 750 Formula and Formula 3 racing cars. Chief officials of the meeting have been found and the general preliminary arrangements are complete,' reported the Bristol club's journal.

However, by February 1956, alarm bells were sounding within the club. Apart from the financial concerns, the after effects of the Le Mans accident were forcing those in charge of the sport to take a long hard look at how spectators were protected at British circuits. A report in the Bristol club's journal of February 1956 commented: 'Circuit racing is usually too expensive for the local member to compete. Apparently a large number of people derive much pleasure from organising these events. We are meeting very shortly to discuss special safety precautions in the light of the RAC report on the International meeting. We hope to meet a Track Inspection Committee from the RAC very shortly at the circuit, and decide with them what additional safety precautions will have to be carried out before the meeting can be put on. We are not in a position to spend a great deal of money on the circuit at the moment.'

The outcome of the meeting with circuit inspectors realised the worst fears of the organisers. Substantial work was required to bring the venue up to the standard now deemed necessary following the Le Mans accident and the club simply could not afford that on top of the loss it had made over the October meeting. Autosport of March 9 carried the sad news: 'The Bristol MC&LCC announce with regret that their proposed race meeting at Castle Combe circuit on 7 April will not take place. This is due to the cost of the safety measures now being requested by the RAC, together with the short time available for their incorporation. The club unfortunately sustained a loss of some £700 on the October meeting last year, and this, together with the cost of necessary safety measures for the coming season, has crippled hopes of an early season meeting. In its desire to continue the promotion of race meetings to satisfy enthusiasts and drivers in the West, the club is hoping that outside assistance can be found to help them organise the meeting normally run during the first week in October.'

But that help was not forthcoming and in late May came a further blow to supporters of the circuit with a further Autosport report. 'The following statement was recently issued by the Castle Combe Committee of the Bristol MC&LCC. "It was decided at the club General Meeting on 17 April to ratify the recommendation of the Castle Combe Committee to cancel the race meeting at the circuit on 6 October. The main cause of this decision was the very high cost of the provision of the safety precautions required by the RAC, and the fact that the club lost a considerable sum of money on the International meeting last October. We are fully aware that spectator safety precautions are advisable, but at the same time, recent events on other circuits have suggested that in their present form they may endanger the safety of drivers. If this should prove to be so, the existing requirements may have to come under review again at a later date. In this event it may well be ill-advised to spend a large sum of money at present. The Committee has spent a great deal of time, and a lot of work has been done by its members, in an effort to explore every avenue before coming to the decision to cancel the event. But unless some sponsorship or other means of raising capital can be found, it is not possible to proceed with plans for future large scale meetings for the present. In the meantime we hope to use the circuit for some of our closed to club events.'"

Following that announcement came the final news that motor racing would, for the foreseeable future at least, be absent from Castle Combe. Autocar magazine of August 24 carried the report. 'The Bristol MC&LCC has announced with regret that, at a club general meeting held on August 14, it was decided to terminate the lease of Castle Combe circuit, and to relinquish all racing rights. The main cause for this decision is the very high cost of providing spectator safety precautions, and the track repairs which would have been necessary before racing could take place again.'

Chris Bigwood recalls the major factors that led to these decisions. 'The earth banks that would have been needed would have precluded the farmer from carrying out his farming. There was no way we could circumvent it. The expense was beyond us at that time.'

Mike Hailwood in the paddock, 1957.

Mike Hailwood (NSU) on his way to victory, 1958.
Photo: Mortons Motorcycle Media.

The epitome of Castle Combe in the 1950s. Ken Wharton at speed in the BRM.
Photo: LAT.

10,000. The revelation of the day was 17 year-old Mike Hailwood who took his MV to fourth in 125 race. Five days earlier he had made his road racing debut at Oulton Park and he would later make his 250cc debut at Castle Combe before going on to dominate the class at world level. Bob Anderson raced a Norton 350 to win the Junior final that day in April and a 500cc version to win the Senior final from Geoff Tanner (Norton). Like Hailwood, Anderson would later make the switch to Grand Prix racing on four wheels as a private entrant.

'The 1955 Le Mans disaster had a catastrophic effect on the sport. The RAC, quite rightly, insisted that you had to have the minimum safety system installed. Strangely enough, not that many places closed as a result but the picture changed over the next four or five years. From 1956 to 1961 the circuit was closed for car racing, but it became an enormous motorcycle venue. The circuit went on hosting testing and sprints as well,' said Strawford.

Although time had been called on car racing, motorbike racing continued largely unaffected by the safety issues of the day. In 1956, the July National meeting went ahead on a wet day with spectator enclosures all round the circuit. One of the highlights was the sidecar race which produced an exciting dice between the Nortons of F Taylor and Bill Boddice until the last lap when Boddice's plug began to pre-ignite and he dropped back to fifth. Another notable winner that day was Derek Minter on a 125 Augusta.

The following year was marked by a pair of motorcycle meetings, with a national event in April drawing a crowd estimated at being between 8000 and

In July, Hailwood was again in the thick of the action, but it was Alastair King who grabbed the headlines. Following an easy 350 win, he chased Geoff Tanner home on the 500 final and broke Surtees' lap record in the process. King pared eight tenths of a second from the two year-old record to leave it at 1m17.2s, an average speed of 85.79mph.

Meetings in April and July were also run in 1958 with Hailwood taking easy wins in the 125 and 250cc races. The line up for the Junior final was crammed with talent and the race finished with Derek Minter beating Bob Anderson and Phil Read with Hailwood sixth. Minter added a further win in the Senior 500 final while Read also won the 350cc race for non-experts. In July, Hailwood won four times, including the Avon Silver Trophy, which was a 15-lap handicap for fastest from the 250, 350 and 500 races. A Motor Cycling report of the race commented: 'The handicaps had been worked out on times recorded on a dry circuit and the rain played havoc with the timekeepers calculations.' However, the fact that Hailwood was a runaway winner was never in doubt.

A soaking day with rain being driven horizontally across the circuit greeted competitors and spectators for the April 1959 national meeting. 'Heavy rain and a strong gusty wind made parts of the course treacherous. The organisers decided to abandon the sidecar handicap towards the end of the programme, but after receiving a deputation from riders were forced to promote another sidecar scratch race,' said the Bristol Evening Post report of the day. Bill Boddice won both sidecar races while Hailwood and Minter both took two wins.

Closing Castle Combe's race programme of the 1950s and bringing to an end the first decade of motorsport at the venue was the July National motorcycle meeting. Like previous events, Hailwood was almost unstoppable and won four races. While he won the Senior 500 race comfortably from the Nortons of John Holder and Tony Godfrey, the latter at least took consolation in equalling King's two year-old circuit record.

Chapter 4

Howard Strawford

-

his early years

For more than 30 of its 50 years, the story of Castle Combe is inextricably linked to that of Howard Strawford. The expatriate Welshman can be blunt, bluff and is unlikely to suffer fools gladly. Underneath though, is a man with a great sense of humour and a true passion for the sport who has given so much of himself to make Castle Combe the success that it has become. In reality, the story is not just of Howard, but of all his whole family. Just as much work has been put in over the years by his long-suffering wife Pat and their daughters Karen and Emma also play significant roles.

The Strawford story dates back to early attempts to get motor racing going in post-war South Wales. 'I was first introduced to motor sport via the Welsh Motor Racing Club, which ran with events at Fairwood. I had recently left school and started an apprenticeship working with my father in a café in Wales. One of our customers was Cyril Clode who talked to my father, who was a great enthusiast, about joining the Welsh Motor Racing Club,' recalls Strawford.

'He persuaded my father to join the club, which was probably a fiver at the time, and they soon got going. There was a big piece in the local papers that they were looking for volunteers to lay out this circuit that they were thinking about at Fairwood. Being the pratt of a volunteer that I was, I volunteered and went up at weekends. And, I thought it was quite brilliant because I was able to go to the racing for nothing. I worked for about six weekends on it and that was my introduction to motor sport. That was around 1952, which was the first

meeting there. I saw my hero, Stirling Moss, have a big accident there. Right in front of me,' he recalls.

Inspired by this first taste of motorsport, it was not long before Howard resolved to try it out for himself. 'As soon as I was old enough I bought a car and joined a motor club. The first thing I ever went to was a hillclimb at a place called Castel Farm. I went with my best friend I met from my days of ballroom dancing, David Evans, and effectively it was a grand prix all the way from Swansea to Castel Farm and back! I just about managed to hang on to his exhaust pipes. The blind date that I took to the hillclimb had been navigating for me and we've never stopped arguing since!' That was his introduction to Pat and it was the beginning of a partnership that would last a lifetime.

'I had a Morgan first of all. But there was a great risk of me blowing the bottom end out of it, the way I was driving it,' he says. 'I decided to pension it off and I got an MG TC. I started sprinting quite successfully. Swansea Motor Club was very much a one town club. We did everything. In fact, it was a joint car and motor cycle club and we were involved in all sorts of things, sixteen or eighteen events a year. Mainly rallies. I celebrated our first anniversary of joining the Swansea Motor Club by asking them to run a rally which within twelve months I was organising. I sort of got into the habit of it,' he says.

'Within a year or so, I joined the committee and within five years I became the Chairman, and took them on to

The circuit as it was when Howard Strawford first crossed the Bristol channel.

Photo: Gordon Francis.

eventually buying the leasehold of Castel Farm. But at the first meeting we celebrated there, one of our friends was killed and that really put the dampers on it. It was also the same weekend that Llandow was opening and obviously Llandow seemed to be the best thing since sliced bread. It was at that time,' he says, remembering the bumpy airfield circuit near Llantwit Major. Before the war Llandow had been Wales' airport.

Although short on facilities, it was a permanent venue of sorts and hosted numerous race meetings through the 1960s and 1970s before eventually closing its doors to racing. 'Yes, it was an awful place really, but there we

are! And as one does, one progressed through the sport. I was a founder member of Welsh Association of Motor Clubs, would you believe. Then I started stewarding kart racing for the RAC and went on to stewarding other things. By coincidence, I had started stewarding race meetings at Llandow, which is why I was probably one of the most experienced organisers in Wales,' says Strawford.

'I think I should put it down on record that I am responsible for opening Llandow. I got it off the RAF first of all and ran the first event there. In the days when they weren't so fussy, I used to compete as well as organise. That was in 1959. The following year we ran a very big sprint there, around the perimeter track and around the numerous roads it had. But unfortunately, it was to be decommissioned. Which is the reason it's got such excellent buildings albeit they're all on the wrong bit as far as the circuit goes. And as a result of it being effectively the best facility in Wales as far as the RAF were concerned, they hung on to it a bit longer. In the meanwhile Rhoose was converted, into Cardiff International Airport. Llandow was a far superior place but they decided to decommission it.'

'When they did though, aided and abetted by somebody with a lot more business sense than me, we put together a consortium to try and buy a section of it. But the deeds of the property when they bought it were set up so that if it ever closed as an airport, all the rights of way would be reinstated. So you had this 500 acre airfield that was cut into five different pieces and completely spoilt from a motor sports point of view. The only way that you could make a circuit out of it was using the main runway, a link to the perimeter, down to the bottom and establish a link back onto the main runway which is why it ended up as such an odd shape.

'I still think there would have been a facility there to this day if they'd run it a bit better, but that's a moot point. I'm delighted to have been associated with the fact that Swansea Motor Club actually went along and bid at the auction. To say that I was naïve as far as property was concerned, would be a minor under-estimation. At the time I'd been running the family business for some time but the redevelopment of Swansea after the war moved the business area away from where we were and so we eventually sold the café business,' he explains.

'After dabbling in the motor industry for a little while, I ran a section of a motor factors business which made number plates and remould tyres. Then I worked for ten years for Kraft Foods and got numerous minuscule promotions. I became an area manager, account manager and numerous other things until eventually they built the Severn bridge in 1967.

'I was one of the many, many people who went to a sales conference at Kraft Foods at the depot in Cardiff, who was told that the bridge would not injure our jobs in

any way, just improve the servicing. In fact they closed it down and sacked everybody. The day before they did it, they promoted me. The promotion was to move over to Bristol and that move brought to the end a run of about three or four years of being chairman of the Swansea Motor Club.'

Moving to Bristol would, ultimately, change his life completely, for it would not be long before he got involved in the running of events at Castle Combe.

Chapter 5

The 1960s

-

the AFN years

As the new decade dawned, it was pretty much business as usual at Castle Combe. Motorcycle racing provided the two main events of the year, with a few sprints and test days added in. Five years on from the last meeting there was, however, some hope for a return of car racing to Wiltshire. Behind the scenes, Nick Syrett of the British Racing and Sports Car Club was about to start negotiating towards a return of car meetings.

As had been the case in 1959, Mike Hailwood and Derek Minter dominated the April national motorcycle meeting and Bill Boddice was the man to beat in sidecar races. Hailwood bagged the 125 and 250cc races while Minter beat off the challenge of Phil Read to win the 500cc final. In the process he lopped a massive 2.2 seconds from the previous circuit record and nudged the mark up towards 90mph with a best lap of 1m15.0s. However, the race of the day was the 350 final which featured a cracking dice between Hailwood's AJS and the Nortons of Minter and Read. Hailwood trailed Minter for much of the race but swept ahead in the last 50 yards to win by a length.

It was a case of more of the same in July for the National Avon Trophy motorcycle meeting. Three wins for Hailwood headlined the meeting although Read took a fine victory in a thrilling 350 final. By 1961 Hailwood had joined the works Honda team and was to win his first world championship, the 250, that year. But in May he was racing at Castle Combe once more and won twice. The 350cc non-experts race was televised and was

probably the first motorbike race to be filmed at the circuit. Despite heavy rain, a close race was won by the Norton of M Uphill. The sidecar final was also televised and was won by MJ Rowell/AG Holtham (Norton).

In July, the national meeting ran in contrasting weather with brilliant sunshine alternating with heavy showers and a violent electrical storm. 'We nearly lost our chief marshal, Bob Giles. One flash of lightning was so near it bowled him over and he was quite dazed for a short time,' read the report in the Wessex Centre ACU Gazette. Hailwood and Minter still did the bulk of the winning while Pip Harris won two sidecar events with his BMW and set the first ever over 80mph lap for a sidecar.

'In 1961 following a considerable amount of negotiation, Nick Syrett of the BRSCC, arranged for the safety system to be paid for by the BRSCC. It was only really a case of digging a bank all the way round. It wasn't really a big deal. So the circuit was re-opened in 1962. Unfortunately, it hadn't been resurfaced and before long the tarmac was breaking up. By now the estate was effectively penniless,' says Strawford.

With the BRSCC footing the bill, the necessary safety work was carried out in time for the club to run three car meetings in 1962. The first meeting of 1962 was the May national motorcycle meeting when Minter and Boddice were again at the head of the action. Also getting noticed was a local rider called Terry Sanger, who was increasing his experience in the 350 non-experts race.

John Dangerfield
(AC Ace) on the
limit, June 1962.

Photo:
Ferret Fotographics.

July 1962: Chris
Summers sets a
new circuit record
in his Cooper
Chevrolet.

Photo:
Ferret Fotographics.

John Taylor about
to spin in 1962.

Photo:
Ferret Fotographics.

Several seasons earlier, Sanger had survived unscathed after a bizarre incident while racing motor cycles. 'One of my earliest memories was riding the BSA Gold Star at Castle Combe,' he recalls. 'I was always too heavy, really, but I was usually first away at the start because I could start it after two or three steps. But that meant I had to be the first to put the brakes on. One of the funniest moments was when I came down to Camp on about the third lap. We were all trying to be the last of the late brakers and I braked far too late. Being heavy, I went clean over the handle bars and I was sat on my backside still doing about 70mph with the bike right behind me, following a straight line off the corner.

'In those days, fifteen feet from the edge of the road were steel posts driven into the ground with a rope stretched between them. The spectators stood behind that and they gently held the rope up as I slid underneath it. But I kept going and by this time my behind was getting a bit sore. I actually went feet first into the Red Cross tent. Ray Cordy, from Bristol, was already in there because he'd fallen off at the start. He looked down at me as I went sliding past and out the other end of the tent. He said: 'You'd better deal with him first, he's in a hurry!'

On June 10, the circuit finally re-opened for car racing when the BRSCC ran a five-race meeting in front of a large crowd on Whit Saturday. First winner of the day was Peter Deal (Lotus 7), followed by Ken Baker (Jaguar E Type), Roy Pierpoint (Lotus Climax), Chris Summers (Cooper Chevrolet), Doc Merfield (Ford Anglia) and Mike Johnson (Lotus Elite). The circuit was formally re-opened by Bob Gerard who ran some demonstration laps in the Formula 1 Cooper he now entered for John Taylor. Later in the day, Taylor took the car over for the Formula Libre race and finished right behind the 4.6-litre engined Cooper of Summers. In the process, Taylor lowered Schell's seven year-old lap record by a second and a half to establish a new record of 1m12.0s, 92.00mph.

In July, both two and four-wheeled meetings were held although the motorbike meeting on July 21 was marred when Michael Brixey from Shepton Mallet was killed after crashing at Camp in practice. Although it was the last time at Castle Combe for Hailwood, it was Minter who took the major spoils with a brace of wins

and a new lap record in 1m13.6s, just a whisker shy of a 90mph average.

Two weeks earlier, the BRSCC car meeting had been notable for another new circuit record when Chris Summers lapped his brutish Cooper Chevrolet in 1m11.2s. The GT race, meanwhile, was again won by Baker but featured Bath garage owner Ron Fry in fourth place in his Ferrari 250GT. If spectators thought that Summers' new record that day was impressive, it paled into insignificance when the final meeting of the season was held on September 8. Despite concerns about the track surface, Summers smashed his own record when he stormed around in 1m09.2s, the first ever sub-1m10s lap and an average speed of 95.72mph. Initially, BRSCC meetings were run by Syrett and Dennis Southwood from the BRSCC headquarters. But the re-opening of the circuit for cars encouraged the formation of the south-western centre of the BRSCC and increasingly local officials took control of the race meetings.

The 1962 season also brought a new racing school to Castle Combe. Roland Dutt, a racer of the era, ran an operation rather grandly called the Vanderbyl Motor Racing Instructional School. The school made use of Elva Mk5 sports-racing cars and assistant instructors were Ray Merrick and David Murray. Three years earlier, an operation called Motor Racing Enterprises had offered lessons in a Cooper-Climax for about four pounds.

The problem of the surface meant that, after just one season and three meetings, car racing once again came to a halt. Autosport carried the news: 'Because of the state of the surface and one or two other points the RAC will not allow further racing at Castle Combe. The BRSCC who were to have held three meetings this year, hope to resurface, improve and alter Castle Combe to RAC requirements so that racing can be resumed there in 1964.'

But the motorcycle events continued and two meetings in 1963 ran in April and July. The April meeting was run in very wet conditions and although he arrived at the circuit, Minter elected not to race because of the conditions. Tom Phillips won twice that day. In July, Gordon Pill suffered a serious accident in practice and later succumbed to his injuries. Later in the day Phillips

Dave Simmonds on the 125cc Tohatsu.
Photo: Mortons Motorcycle Media.

again won twice, as did Dave Simmonds on two of the rare Tohatsu machines. Having come to prominence with the Japanese company competing on a 50cc version, Dave and his brother Mike were given a pair of 125cc machines by the Tohatsu company. It was at that July 1963 meeting at Castle Combe that they really made their mark, as Dave won both the 50cc and the 125cc race. Beating Hailwood's 125cc lap record was a real bonus and helped Dave towards a Grand Prix debut with Tohatsu.

'One of the most significant things of the 1960s was the appearance of Dave Simmonds,' says motorcycle commentator Andy Blackman. 'He was relatively well-known but the Tohatsu bike was completely unknown and the first time he raced it at Castle Combe he smashed Hailwood's 125cc lap record.' However, hopes that this would lead to a Grand Prix campaign with Tohatsu were dashed when the Japanese firm went bust before the 1964 season. Like many others who raced on two wheels at Castle Combe in their early years, Simmonds went on to become the 1969 125cc world champion.

Blackman's passion for motorcycle racing had come about purely by chance. 'I discovered the circuit and the sport by accident. I was a keen boxer and I used to cycle

for fitness. I happened to cycle down West Way one day, totally unaware that there was a circuit there, and there was a meeting on. I went down as far as Tower and climbed over the fence. That's how I discovered the sport. I didn't race at Castle Combe that often. I got to know Jack Harding, the well-known scrutineer, and when I wasn't riding, I used to go to the circuit as a scrutineer. In the 1960s the racing scene was very much on a national basis. We didn't run club events, it was part of the national calendar and all the major stars of national and international racing came to Castle Combe. Riders like Derek Minter, Phil Read and Bill Ivy were all very much part of that,' he recalls.

As the 1963 season drew to a close, the management of the circuit was about to change. AFN, better known as the company behind Frazer Nash was linked to the circuit by the friendship between Kitty Thomas and AFN boss Harold John Aldington or HJ as he was known. Late in 1963 AFN Ltd took a lease on the circuit and AFN (Castle Combe) Ltd was formed by HJ's son, John Aldington.

The circuit was resurfaced by early April 1964 and was, according to Autosport, as smooth as a billiard table. However, it seems that this was perhaps not as comprehensive a job as contemporary reports suggested, as the circuit would need to be resurfaced again within just three years. Spectator facilities were also improved, with viewing at all but one corner. Quarry Corner was again open to the public after the safety bank had been built and other improvements were made to the paddock and adjacent buildings.

However, the return of car racing and the resurfacing work did not sit well with all users and caused some friction with the Wessex Centre of the ACU. Its gazette of September 1963 voiced some concerns: 'Our agreement over the circuit has now expired and the chances of a new one has many difficulties, the most important one being that, to date, the Centre has footed the bill for any repairs that have been done, while many others have used the course without doing anything to

The king of the Castle. Howard Strawford, the man who made it happen.

Ayrton Senna da Silva heads the Formula Ford 2000 pack into Quarry, 1982.

Photo: John Gaisford.

Senna powers his Van Diemen RF82 through Tower.

Photo: John Gaisford.

Vince Woodman's Cologne Capri in action, April 1985.

September 1985.
Johnny Herbert (6)
lines up on the
Formula Ford grid
ahead of Damon
Hill.

Photo:
John Gaisford.

Herbert heads
Kevin Gillen and
Mark Blundell,
September 1985.

Photo:
John Gaisford.

Belgian Bertrand
Gachot guides his
Van Diemen RF85
through Camp.

Photo:
John Gaisford.

In the spring of 1989 the pit road was constructed with a spot of help from hands-on management.

Photo: John Gaisford.

May 1989. David Coulthard and Kelvin Burt head the Junior Formula Ford pack through Quarry.
Photo: John Gaisford.

Formula 1 action at Quarry, April 1990.

Photo: Paul Korkus.

The circuit was completely resurfaced in November 1992.

Photo: John Gaisford.

Although touring car racing has not featured at the circuit, the cars have tested there. This is Kelvin Burt's works Ford Mondeo.

Nick Mason poses with his Ferrari 250GTO on the startline.

Alan Cooper oversees another racing school day.

Photo: John Gaisford.

August 1993. Prince Michael of Kent (left) and Lord Montagu (right).

A 1993 Formula Ford pack lines up on the grid in front of race control.

'Just about breaking even that day,' says Strawford of this 1993 crowd at Quarry.

Motorbike track days - one of the growth industries of the 1990s.

Photo: Colin Allgood.

Gavin Wills, four times Formula Ford champion.

Photo: Steve Jones.

A 1994 Mini Miglia pack is filmed through Folly.

Formula Ford 1600 has thrilled Castle Combe crowds for more than 30 years. Gavin Wills heads the pack.

Photo:
Steve Jones.

Ferraris get confused at Camp in 1997.

Richard Carter locks a wheel ahead of the Formula Ford pack at Quarry.

Photo: Steve Jones.

August 1997. The TVR Tuscan pack fans out on the charge down Farm Straight.

The Special GT pack storms through Folly.

Tiff Needell demonstrates the Lotus 49 at the Classic Meeting in August 1997.

Nigel Greensall setting the fastest lap ever recorded at Castle Combe, August 1997.

Photo: Steve Jones.

Historic Road Sports stream into Old Paddock, August 1997.

Photo: Steve Jones.

keep the course in order. To put things bluntly, the Centre has carried or kept the circuit going for their own benefit, but as the car people say, we have had the wrong end of the stick, but they are unable to help.'

The 1964 programme kicked off on April 18 with the first of three national motorcycle meetings. In late June was the first of five car meetings, with the BRSCC running the re-opening meeting. In mid-August the BRSCC ran its second meeting while, for the first time, other dates were taken by the Austin Healey Car Club/750 Motor Club, the Hagley and District Light Car Club and the Sevenoaks and District Motor Club. It was the busiest season to date for the circuit.

On two wheels it was the year of Dave Simmonds and his Tohatsu who continued to dominate the 50cc events. Minter was also a frequent victor and was one of three riders to hold the outright circuit record during the 1964 season. In April, Tom Phillips made good use of the improved track surface to set the first ever 90mph lap when he took his 500cc Norton round in 1m13.0s. In hot July sunshine, Minter topped that by four-tenths of a second while in September Chris Conn equalled that lap. But perhaps the most significant thing about the September event was Bill Ivy's victory in the 125cc race when he was a last-minute rider nomination on the Chisholm Honda Special and charged through from the back of the grid to win the race.

The increased speed from the new surface was best demonstrated when the opening car meeting was held on June 27. Airline pilot Hugh Dibley slashed nearly three seconds from the two year-old standard of Chris Summers to leave the record tantalisingly close to the 100mph mark. In his Coventry Climax powered Brabham BT8 sports-racer, Dibley saw off the challenge of Roy Pierpoint in the brutish Attila Chevrolet to win the Sports-Racing Car event and set a new lap record in 1m6.4s, an average speed of 99.76mph. Other notable winners that day included Ron Fry (Ferrari 250GTO) and Roger Swanton who kept his Lotus Cortina just ahead of Ted Williams' Ford Anglia in a cracking over 1000cc Saloon Car race.

In July, the Austin Healey and 750 clubs jointly ran a meeting that was badly delayed by early morning mist. Sadly, once the racing got underway, Bob Beck crashed

his Lola single-seater into the marshals' post on the inside at Old Paddock and later died in hospital as a result of his injuries. A month later the BRSCC was back at the helm with a meeting notable for several names who would later go on to become familiar in the sport. Peter Gethin, who won the 1971 Italian Grand Prix for BRM, started the GT event from the front row of the grid in his Lotus 23 but retired from the race. Second place in the 1000cc sports car race, meanwhile, went to the Lotus 7 of Maurice Phillippe, who would later design grand prix cars for Colin Chapman's Lotus team.

After the Sevenoaks club ran a meeting in August, the season concluded with the first of what would become a regular series of race meetings run by the midlands-based Hagley club. That October event was headlined by the over 1000cc saloon car race in which Robin Smith (Lotus Cortina) saw off the Mini Coopers of John Handley (Broadspeed) and Steve Neal (Arden).

On the back of a successful 1964 season, an even bigger programme was planned for 1965 with eleven car meetings and four motorcycle events. There would have been a twelfth car event had the 750 Motor Club meeting planned for June not been cancelled due to lack of entries. New organising clubs for the car events were AFN, the British Automobile Racing Club and the Vintage Sports Car Club. The event in May organised by Michael Burn for AFN was primarily for Saab, Porsche, Lancia and Frazer Nash cars and included races, high speed trials, an hour-long handicap relay race and a sprint. For the relay race, pits were built on the inside of the track just after the start/finish line and it was won by the Frazer Nash team which completed 40 laps.

Apart from Ron Fry, who raced both his Ferrari 250LM and a Mini Cooper and earned the 'King of Combe' tag, other local names were coming to the fore including Vince Woodman (Lotus Cortina), Geoff Mabbs (Janspeed Cooper S) and David George (Mini Cooper S). Thirty years later, George would still be a regular visitor to the circuit as lead race commentator. He also featured in one of the best dices of the season when, at the August Sevenoaks & DMC meeting, he was part of a five-car battle for the lead of the up to 1000cc saloon car race. Mike Campbell-Cole (Mini Cooper) and Roger Nathan (Hillman Imp) were amongst his rivals.

June 1964: Bob Rose escaped unharmed after rolling his Marcos at Quarry.
Photo: Ferret Fotographics.

In September, the VSCC ran an 11-race meeting for vintage and Edwardian cars and the historic racing car event was won by John Spero in a Maserati 250F thought to be an ex-Horace Gould car. If that were the car, it seems certain to have been the car that Gould raced to second in the Avon Trophy Formula 1 race 10 years previously. Wrapping up the season in October was the second Hagley meeting of the year which was notable for the very first 100mph lap of Castle Combe. Having lost his circuit record to Hugh Dibley in 1964, Chris Summers returned in a 5.4-litre Chevrolet-engined Lotus 24 and won the Formula Libre race at a canter. His best lap of 1m5.2s represented an average speed of 101.59mph.

On two wheels in 1965, riders at the head of the action included Derek Minter, Dave Simmonds, Rod Scivyer, Peter Williams, Ray Whatmore and Dave Croxford. In

the July meeting, Minter also set a new circuit record in 1m12.2s even though carburettor problems slowed his Norton in the closing stages and allowed Whatmore through to win. As they had done in May, during the first meeting, Trevor Davies and Pete Wild won the sidecar race on their Vincent, but a new threat emerged at the July meeting in the form of 17 year-old Mick Boddice, son of Bill, on a Manx Norton.

In July, the longest race ever to be held at the circuit was run when the Southampton Motor Cycle Club held the International Grand Prix d'Endurance. This 500 mile race had been run at Thruxton but by 1965 the runways at the Hampshire venue had gained too many potholes to make racing viable. Instead, for what proved to be a single running of the event it moved to Castle Combe and 45 motorbikes started the race at noon from a Le Mans-type start. Six and a half hours later, after 272 laps, the 650cc Triumph Bonneville of Barry Lawton and Dave Degens took the chequered flag having averaged nearly 80mph through the long afternoon. Elsewhere in the results, local manufacturer Cotton won one of the classes with Derek Minter and Peter Inchley riding a Cotton Conquest. A torrential downpour just after the start lasted for 15 minutes and threatened to disrupt the event, but the track soon dried. A refuelling pits was set up on Farm Straight where a considerable amount of fuel was spilt and later forced the circuit owners to resurface the worst affected patches.

Natalie Goodwin (Lotus 7) in August 1964.

Photo: Ferret Fotographics.

Tony Lanfranchi (Lola T70) is beaten away by Chris Lambert's Brabham F3 car in 1966.

Photo: Gordon Francis.

Geoff Mabbs (here in Jan Odor's Mini) was a regular winner in the 1960s.

Photo: Gordon Francis.

Derek Minter leads Dave Croxford in July 1965.

Photo: Mortons Motorcycle Media.

The field assembles in the paddock, September 1965.

Photo: Dave Vass.

Chris Summers (Lotus 24-Chevrolet) leads Mac Daghorn (Lola T70).

Photo: Gordon Francis.

Saloons in 1966. Brian Cutting leads Vince Woodman, Ron Fry and Steve Neal.

Photo: Gordon Francis.

Ron Fry, the original ' King of Combe' leads Mike Crabtree's Elan in 1966.

Photo: Gordon Francis.

Derek Minter checks on his rivals, July 1966.

Photo: Mortons Motorcycle Media.

While plans for another busy season in 1966 were being laid, signs of local opposition to the circuit were starting to appear again. The Wessex ACU Gazette of December 1965 reported the situation. 'The Calne and Chippenham Rural District Council decided to ban Sunday meetings and impose certain controls including a stipulation that all events should not start earlier than 8am and finish no later than 6.30pm. Miss LD Wright who lives at the Old Smithy, near the circuit, alleged that the conditions gave race organisers as much liberty as before. 'The noise is a danger to health. If it continues we shall all go dotty,' she said. Mrs Thomas said she was very annoyed and accused people of being petty

Peter Gethin and Mike Walker battle at Old Paddock in 1966.

Photo: Gordon Francis.

minded. She said she was going to appeal against the controls. Under the new rulings the season is being limited to 26 Saturdays and three Bank Holidays. Testing is to be limited to three days a week and Sunday use of the track is banned. Use of the public address system is limited to commentary purposes, ruling out the playing of music.'

The circuit was not the only interruption to the quiet Wiltshire countryside that year, however. Film makers from 20th Century Fox took over the village when shooting location scenes for its hit film Dr Doolittle in which Rex Harrison played the starring role as the man able to talk to the animals. The village was converted into

the fictional Puddleby-on-the-Marsh for the occasion and was forever assured streams of tourists as a result.

Back at the race circuit, the calendar for 1966 featured 13 car meetings and three for motorcycles. A fourteenth car meeting scheduled for June was cancelled by the West Hants and Dorset Car Club. The car season started strongly with a reported 15,000 crowd for the BARC meeting on Easter Monday April 11 and was topped by a 15-lap GT race won by Mike De Udy in the latest Porsche 906, who caught and passed early leader Ron Fry (Ferrari 250LM). Fry later took consolation by racing his Mini Cooper S to a saloon car victory.

John Berry leads Hugh Dibley and Peter Clarke during the Hagley 100 in 1966.
Photo: Gordon Francis.

In May, the Frazer Nash and Porsche clubs joined forces to run a race meeting that featured the first race for the Griffiths formula. This race for historic sports cars would later be the catalyst for the creation of the Historic Sports Car Club and was won by Neil Corner's Jaguar D Type. In May, the Hagley club were back in charge and the circuit record was beaten again, this time by Tony Lanfranchi in Sid Taylor's Lola T70. Although he later spun out of the GT race he lowered the record to 1m4.8s but before the afternoon was out he had gone even faster. Having spun at Quarry early in the race, Lanfranchi battled back to win the Hagley Trophy Formula Libre race and trimmed another fifth of a second from the record, leaving it at 1m4.6s (102.54mph).

When the Hagley club ran its second meeting of the season, it featured the Hagley 100 run over 55 laps and equalled the circuit's longest ever car race, the Avon Trophy Formula 1 race of 1955. While others faltered, Max Wilson came through to win in his Brabham BT8 from Ron Fry (Ferrari 250LM) and Geoff Breakell (Brabham BT8). Non-starters were Sid Taylor (Lola T70) and David Prophet (McLaren) while retirements included Hugh Dibley (Lola T70), John Berry (Lotus 40) and Chris Ashmore (Elva 7S).

The motorcycle calendar reverted to a more traditional three meeting format after the experiment of the 1965 endurance race. In April, Williams, Minter and Croxford all featured strongly while Rod Gould (Aermacchi) and Peter Inchley (Villiers Starmaker) were other notable winners. Owen Greenwood, meanwhile, scored a sidecar victory in his controversial Mini Special and broke Bill Boddice's lap record in the process. The Mini Special was a unique but highly-effective self-conceived machine, as Andy Blackman remembers. 'It was based on a Mini subframe which he put on the ground and they sat on the floor with the engine and steering rack. Owen and Terry Fairbrother, his passenger, sat on the floor in the right position and drew chalk lines around them. They then put tubes into position and away they went. It was built in six weeks.

'It caused some controversy because although in those days Morgans and the odd front-wheel drive machine were around, albeit driven by motorcycle engines, they were never particularly competitive. But no one had ever taken much notice of the front-wheel drive option. Greenwood was scratching his head about what to do and the Mini Cooper S was doing all the winning in saloon cars at the time. It offered a cheap engine which was unburstable, unlike the Triumphs he was using.

'He had to have a pusher so he could never start from the front of the grid. But he had so much more power and road-holding because he had two wheels at the front and two at the back. The regulations in those days said that if

John Berry's Lotus 40 during the Hagley 100, August 1966.

Photo: Ferret Fotographics.

Ron Fry (Mini) and
Vince Woodman
(Lotus Cortina)
drift through
Tower.

Photo:
Gordon Francis.

The Hon Patrick
Lindsay (Maserati
250F) heads Jean
Le Sage (Lotus 16)
in a 1966 Historic
race.

Photo:
Gordon Francis.

Alan Rollinson
(Brabham BT21)
sets the pace in
September 1966.

Photo:
Gordon Francis.

Chris Summers also raced a Jaguar E-Type. Here, he leads the similar car of Terry Kirby at Quarry.
Photo: Gordon Francis.

Saloon first lap at Quarry with Geoff Mabbs (right) and Steve Neal at the head of the pack.
Photo: Gordon Francis.

Tony Shaw leads Ron Fry at Easter 1967.

Photo: Peter Rushby.

there was less than six inches between the centres, you could run two wheels on the back. So it was actually a four-wheeler. In the famous photograph of it rolling at Castle Combe in July 1967, a marshal called John Howard is running out from the banking. Howard was still marshalling at the circuit more than 30 years later. That was the only time he ever looped it. They went on to win just about everything with it,' says Blackman.

By the close of the 1966 season, two major problems faced the circuit. Planning permission allied to local pressure was a growing issue and the track surface again needed major attention. 'The track needed resurfacing so John Aldington of AFN got estimates for the work. The price was about £20,000 and he went along to see the bank manager. But the bank manager asked him about the lease and planning permission, both of which were going to run out over the next couple of years. Since the

circuit opened, planning permission had always been renewed on a temporary basis for three years at a time.'

Although a renewal of the lease was only a formality, the thorny subject of planning permission was a much greater concern for Mrs Thomas who continued in the role of circuit manager. 'AFN (Castle Combe) Ltd applied for 21 years' planning permission but the story behind it was leaked. Some local residents saw an opportunity to group together as an objectors' association led by a Mr Griffiths who lived in Upper Castle Combe. The application before Calne and Chippenham Urban District Council was refused in January 1967. Somehow or other, Aldington wrote out a cheque and had it resurfaced, which was just as well as it wouldn't have lasted much longer. Then he more or less wanted to wash his hands of the whole thing,' recalls Strawford.

'AFN said that the present three-year permission did not permit it to make the necessary capital outlay to improve facilities and amenities. The council's planning committee refused permission on the grounds of nuisance to local residents, traffic congestion, and the fact that the area is one of great beauty,' said a contemporary press report. 'The verdict of the council was eight votes to six against, while public support for the application outnumbered the opposition by 1000 to 16. AFN is to appeal to Ministry of Local Housing and Local Government. This will be heard in three or four months' time. Meanwhile racing will continue this year and next under the present planning permission which runs out in November 1968.'

'If they had obtained a certificate of established usage, which would have cost the equivalent of 25p, they wouldn't have needed planning permission. The estate was ill-advised. Mrs Thomas was still running the place and ultimately came up with a plan of applying for planning permission for 21 years. They went to Lincolns Inn Fields and hired one of the most expensive solicitors in the land. Unfortunately, the story got about that if they couldn't tarmac the circuit, it would close down and so local objectors got together to oppose it. They were refused planning,' says Strawford.

'The planning difficulties which face Castle Combe circuit ensure that the costs of hiring, advertising, spectator administration, will remain relatively high. In order that Clubs may balance their budget a certain minimum spectator attendance is necessary. Whilst Bank Holiday attendance is generally sufficient to cover expenses, Saturday racing rarely draws enough spectators,' said a correspondent in Motoring News in June 1967.

However, while the planning wrangles raged on, the 1967 season got underway with 14 car meetings planned but only two motorcycle events. This reduction in two-wheeled competition had been known since the previous autumn and was not well received by the Wessex Centre of the ACU. Its Gazette of September 1966 voiced the feelings of the Centre. 'The cars have pushed us out, AFN (Castle Combe) Ltd has forgotten who kept the circuit going from 1956 to 1964.'

The motorcycle meetings in April and July featured many of the names that had been successful in previous seasons including Peter Inchley, Dave Croxford and Owen Greenwood. In April, Croxford (Matchless) won an exciting 500cc final by half a second from Percy Tait (Triumph), while Croxford and Barry Randle (Norton) jointly equalled Derek Minter's two year old lap record.

Despite snow during morning practice, a record 20,000 crowd turned out at Easter for the opening car meeting of the season run by the BARC. Local stars in the action included Brian Cutting (Ford Anglia), Ron Fry (Ford GT40 and Ford Anglia) and John Chatham (Austin Healey 3000). In May, the BRSCC meeting featured a non-championship Formula 3 race run over two 15-lap parts, with the aggregate result decided on a points basis. Joint winners were Peter Westbury and Derek Bell in a pair of Felday Engineering Brabham BT21s. Also in the field were future Grand Prix racers Tim Schenken (Lotus 22) and Howden Ganley (Brabham BT21).

In July, Mini Cooper racer Fred Brady died after crashing at Camp. In the Clubmans Sports race, future FIA President Max Mosley won in his Mallock U2 while the very first Formula Ford race to be held at Castle Combe was won by Dan Hawkes in a Lotus 51. John Woolfe won the sportscar event in his AC Cobra and Jim Moore won the Formula Libre race in his famous Kincraft single-seater. In the Motoring News GT Championship round, Fry's new Ford GT40 saw off the challenge of John Lepp's Chevron B8. In August the BARC ran its third and last meeting of the season which included, for the first time, a round of the British Formula Vee Championship. Jenny Nadin emerged victorious and would later go on to earn recognition as Jenny Birrell for her role in organising the British Touring Car Championship in the 1990s.

The 1967 also heralded the creation of Formula Ford, a category that would produce countless epic races at Castle Combe for more than 30 years. One early competitor was Richard Mallock in a front-engined car of the type made famous by his father Arthur. 'I was just using a standard Cortina GT engine in a Mallock and after I'd done about five races Ford announced they were going to create the Formula Ford category. My car, less mudguards and with different tyres, complied straight away,' recalls Richard. When the category had its very first race at Brands Hatch in July 1967, the entry comprised 15 Lotus 51s from the racing school, a single Brabham and the Mallock Mk6R. Unfortunately, Richard never made the grid as he claims the dubious honour of being the first person ever to crash a Formula Ford. He went into the bank at Druids on the warming up lap.

'Arthur had said, "You can't race anywhere except Silverstone and Castle Combe until you've done your six races." I think I'd done my six races by then,' recalls Richard. 'The trouble with that situation is that at somewhere like Silverstone if you locked your brakes and went straight on down at Becketts, it didn't matter. You just turned round and came back. So then we went to Brands, I locked the brakes up and went straight into the tyre wall. You only learn if it hurts!'

Arthur was away on holiday at the time and so a sheepish Richard had to ring up and break the news. 'I think I raced at Castle Combe the day before and did some damage there. I was dicing and we went down to Old Paddock. Totally inexperienced, I went on an inside line at the same speed and came out of the corner and understeered onto the grass. I had no seat belt and thought, "Oh my God." I remember sitting down in the seat, holding onto my privates and closing my eyes. I hit the bottom of this bank, rode straight up onto the top of it at about 100mph! I went straight along the top of the bank and back onto the track and got going again,' says Richard. 'Nowadays, with all the circuit safety changes, the car would probably have been written off.' Richard continued to race the Mk6R in Formula Ford for the balance of 1967. He often drove it to the circuits, took the mud-guards off and raced it before, hopefully, driving it home again.

Bringing the curtain down on the 1967 season at Castle Combe was another Hagley meeting in September, which featured an epic Formula Libre race. Hugh Dibley took pole position in a car entered without a name. The Lotus twin-cam engined car was, in fact, the very first in the line of Palliser racing cars that Dibley constructed into the 1970s. When he retired on the opening lap, the two grandees of Libre racing of the era fought out a titanic battle with Jim Moore (Kincraft) beating Chris Summers (Lotus 24).

That 1967 season was also one of the most successful ever for local hero Terry Sanger in his mighty Ford Cortina V8. Having raced extensively on two and four wheels at Castle Combe in the 1950s and 1960s, including driving an AC Ace, a Morgan and a Marcos, Sanger switched to saloon car racing car. For the 1967 season, Sanger raced one of his best known cars when he squeezed a 289ci Ford engine into a Ford Cortina. Doc Merfield had recently taken a similar route to create what was the very first of the special saloons by installing an engine other than the basic production model. 'His car had a Climax V8 engine but mine had a 289 unit. Because of the step of the rear window down to the boot lid, you had a low pressure area if you went quickly. His car just got into the realms of this and got a bit unstable at top speed. I worked at Bristol cars at the time and went to the aerodynamicist for help. He came up with the idea of a scoop underneath the car and a scoop on each side. The radiator was where the back seat should be and then all the air went out through a big hole. They worked it out that the quicker I went, it actually produced downforce! In 1967, it held the saloon lap records just about everywhere, including Castle Combe, although it used to understeer a bit,' he recalls. From there, Sanger acquired a Ford Falcon and raced internationally. He also raced for the works Ford GT40 sportscar team as well as in Formula 5000 single-seaters.

The Castle Combe programme was similar for 1968, with 13 car meetings and now just two for motorcycles. The BRSCC became the most prolific organiser with four meetings to the two events run by the BARC. On two wheels it was an unremarkable season with events in April and July although during the second meeting Dave Croxford took a share of the outright circuit record by becoming the fourth rider to lap in 1m12.2s.

One of the best meetings in the car season was the BRSCC event at the end of May which featured an epic Mini battle between Richard Longman, Jonathan Buncombe and regular Combe ace Vic Crapnell. Renato Bertorelli won a hectic Formula Ford race which started with a multi-car incident at Quarry on the opening lap. In the 25-lap Special GT race that headlined the meeting, Ron Fry again showed himself master of his local track by lapping the entire field in his Ford GT40. However, it was Formula Libre winner Jim Moore who starred as he

Gerry Dobbins gets into trouble in the Fraud Cortina after a clash with Richard Longman, July 1968.
Photo: Hugh Bishop.

fought back from a first lap spin at Quarry. On his way to victory in the 4.7 Ford-engined Kincraft he trimmed a fifth of a second from Tony Lanfranchi's circuit record to set a new standard of 1m4.4s (102.86mph). Despite a brave challenge from John Fenning (Brabham BT21), Moore went on to win convincingly.

Less than two months later, armed with the ex-Dan Gurney lightweight Ford GT40, Fry equalled Moore's new lap record as he recovered from a slow start to take the GT lead from Chris Skeaping's Chevron B8. The over 1000cc Saloon race was incident packed and was finally won by the Ford Anglia of Archie Forbes. But that was only after various dramas had befallen Richard Longman, Terry Sanger (ex-Alan Mann Ford Falcon) and Gerry Dobbins in the Daimler-engined 'Fraud' Cortina which was one of the early examples of the special saloon car that would proliferate in the 1970s. Another Formula Ford thriller was won by Bryan Sharp from the similar Merlyn of Ian Foster and the Brabham of Tony Trimmer.

While the 1968 racing season was in full swing, the planning inquiry was finally held in May. The local planning inspector recommended a 20-year permission for 19 meetings per year between March and October, but no international meetings. But the Minister, Anthony Greenwood, over-ruled that recommendation in October and allowed merely another three years' planning from the start of 1969 and stated that an alternative site should be found when the new permission ran out at the end of 1971. It was, effectively, an order to close Castle Combe circuit.

'In the Minister's opinion the aim should be for the use to be discontinued within a reasonable period which will give the appellants time to transfer their activities elsewhere if they so desire,' quoted the verdict from the minister. 'It went to appeal and again AFN used a flash London solicitor to come down to the country and talk to the peasants! It was not well received and they lost. AFN, which had gone ahead with the resurfacing and hired solicitors Vivash Robinson & Company, was somewhat upset. This caused friction to start between AFN and Mrs

John Fenning (Brabham BT21), July 1968.

Photo: Hugh Bishop.

Thomas, who suspected that local solicitors would have done much better. It was suggested that the circuit should close down in three years time at the end of 1971 and move to more suitable premises. Fortunately, it also said that the local authority should help with this move,' says Strawford.

The other notable event of 1968 was the arrival of Pat and Howard Strawford to take over the role of competition secretary for the South Western centre of the BRSCC. 'When we moved to Bristol, I thought I'd retire from organising, but I got that wrong. I didn't like the DIY much. I came to Castle Combe as RAC Steward for BRSCC in late September 1967.

'I'd been to look at the circuit when we moved in, but I couldn't actually find it. I couldn't understand what all the fuss was about because I couldn't find it. It wasn't in use very much then. We'd stayed in the area before, because I competed a number of times at Dyrham Park. In the last couple of years, while we were still in

Swansea, we started a family. Our first daughter Karen was born, and that pulled the budget strings so hard that that was the end of competing! I was exceptionally well looked after by the BRSCC's chief marshal at the time, Philip Boobyer, and he encouraged me to come to the next meeting and to come to the social events with him.

'I went back three or four times as club steward, when I wasn't appointed RAC steward. In November 1968 I was astonished to get a call at the front door from David Wyatt, who was chairman of the centre, to ask if I was interested in joining the committee and being the competition secretary. And stupid me, I said 'Yes'. This involved working with Mrs Thomas quite extensively. We argued a lot but we drank a lot as well!' recalls Strawford. But that wasn't the only change on the horizon.

'John Aldington was a gentleman farmer and didn't really share our enthusiasm for the sport and he could see no future for the place. He was approached by John

Colin Vandervell's Merlyn Mk11 Formula Ford, August 1969.

Photo: Ferret Fotographics.

John Turner leads Ray Payne in a Hillman Imp contest, August 1969.

Photo: Ferret Fotographics.

Webb of Motor Circuit Developments, who took a sub-lease on the circuit for £7000 a year over a three-year period from 1969 to 1971,' says Strawford.

Aldington's deal with Webb, however, was not universally well received. More than anyone, Mrs Thomas was very upset by the arrangement. Her mother had recently died and she had finally inherited the estate from the trust. To avoid potential death duties, she quickly signed most of the land over to her son Paul, and retained only the circuit and a 30 foot strip on either side, plus the paddock and car park down towards Tower. The deal with MCD ended her day to day activity in relation

to a circuit that she had done so much to keep going over the years. Publicly, at least, she attributed her decision to the on-going planning battles and announced that she was going to emigrate to Cyprus.

'I have been driven out by all the opposition. This decision has been boiling up inside me ever since the planning application for the future of the circuit was refused,' she said at the time. 'John Aldington claimed to Mrs Thomas, who was very upset by the move, that John Webb had agreed to endeavour to settle the planning problems,' explains Strawford.

By August of 1969, there was a glimmer of hope for the future, but it was in fact only a technicality. 'AFN (Castle Combe) Ltd has won the High Court appeal against the Ministerial decision to close Combe in three years time. The original ruling was quashed and AFN awarded costs because of a technical error in the presentation of the case by the Minister's inspector that stated the circuit was only used for car testing from March until October. This is untrue but it does not mean a reprieve. All the Minister has to do now is re-issue his original ruling with accurate substantiating evidence,' quoted a press report of late August. This was duly done, and the 1971 closure once again hung over the circuit.

Most enthusiasts and competitors now accepted that the circuit had only three seasons of competition left and the 1969 programme included 12 car meetings and two motorcycle meetings. Showing the increasing involvement of the Strawfords and the BRSCC, five of the car meetings were now run by the club.

'Effectively I got pushed into being competition secretary at the BRSCC and came to this without any real understanding of what was involved. But, of course, it was before championships were common and so we would have two saloon car races and a Formula Libre race. The championship allocations for the BRSCC were so sparse that all we got given that year was the Gregor Grant Clubmans Championship. We had a round of it at every meeting in 1969 which to this day is the reason why I am known to people like Max Mosley, the late Harvey Postlethwaite, Jeremy Lord and Patrick McNally. Some of the most desperately influential people in the sport came from that championship,' says Strawford.

'I was the first person in the country to come up with the idea of having a regional championship,' reckons Strawford. 'I applied directly to the RAC for the Formula Ford championship for 1969. By chance someone I knew from South Wales had moved across to this area and was in charge of advertising for Guards cigarettes. So we started off with sponsorship from Guards. I thought we could generate enough interest in the area for it to work.' His forward thinking was to kick off one of the most successful of all regional championships and start a trend that would form a mainstay of Castle Combe race

meetings for more than 30 years. The full story of the circuit-based championships will be found in chapter 11.

The first car meeting of 1969 featured two heats and a final for Saloons and, driving both a 1000cc and 1300cc Mini, Richard Longman won both heats before winning the 20-lap final in the more powerful of the pair of Downton Engineering cars. His three wins netted Longman £130 in prize money. The BARC's only meeting of the season was on a wet day in May but was notable for the 1000cc Saloon car race which was won by Bill McGovern's Hillman Imp from John Peachey-Austin (Mini Cooper) and Roger Williamson (Ford Anglia). An easy winner of the Motoring News Special GT race was David Purley (Chevron B8) and just four years later both Williamson and Purley would be racing in grands prix.

In other races from the 1969 season, notable victors included John Manners (Mini Cooper), Jeremy Lord (U2 Mk6), Chris Inch (Mini Cooper), Brian Cutting (Ford Mustang) and Terry Sanger (Ford Falcon). On two wheels, April and July meetings heralded rounds of the Auto Cycle Union championships but it was a young 18 year-old on his first visit to Castle Combe who made the headlines in the July meeting. A commanding victory in the 125cc race went to young Barry Sheene on his Bultaco, and suggested that he could have a bright future in the sport.

In October, the final car meeting of the decade was organised by the Hagley club amidst growing pessimism that motor racing at Castle Combe had but two years left.

Chapter 6

The 1970s

-

Strawford steps in

The 1970 season opened with more news about the likely future for the circuit. AFN announced plans to develop the site for offices, storage and a test track with race days limited to just five each year.

'Although the circuit was due to close at the end of 1971, I spoke to the BRSCC locally, Mrs Thomas and John Aldington about trying to do something about the future. At about this time, Aldington sold AFN. Porsche wanted to build this enormous place in the paddock area and have a test track on site. But as part of that, they indicated that they would be prepared to reduce the number of race meetings to five a year. The circuit had been holding as many as 20 meetings. Eventually a deal was struck that if they signed away the rights to run more than five meetings a year, the planners would recommend the building. But as well as recommending it, they also took it to the planning committee and made sure it didn't go through,' says Strawford.

Although he could not have realised it at the time, Howard Strawford had taken the first steps on a journey that would occupy much of his time, energy and waking life for more than 20 years. To show his commitment to the cause, he also took over as Clerk of the Course for the BRSCC South Western centre in May 1970 for the Formula 5000 meeting.

Heading into what seemed certain to be the penultimate season, a programme of 14 car races and two motorcycle events were again scheduled for 1970. The BRSCC was now running six of the car meetings with others hosted by the BARC, the Hagley club, the 750MC, the Monoposto Racing Club and the MG Car Club. The season started earlier than ever before with the first BRSCC meeting on 14 March. Andy Rouse won a single-seater race in his Formula Ford Dulon LD4C while Australian hopefuls Brian McGuire and future World Champion Alan Jones also featured in the entry.

In April, the 19 year-old Ray Mallock won a Clubmans race in a U2 Mk8B created by his father Arthur. Racing a similar car was Harvey Postlethwaite who would go on to design leading grand prix cars. At the same meeting, the over 1300cc Saloon car race was won by the famous 'Run Baby Run' Ford Escort of Dave Brodie who saw off the challenge of Gerry Marshall (Vauxhall Viva GT) and Martin Birrane (7-litre Ford Fairlane). But the highlight of the season was on 9 May when a round of the Guards European Formula 5000 Championship marked one of the most important and prestigious races that the circuit would ever host.

The race was run in two parts and even during qualifying there was little doubt that the circuit record book was going to be re-written. But even the experts were stunned when the 5-litre Chevrolet powered monsters smashed the record to pieces and set a new standard that would remain untouched for 14 years. When Peter Gethin and Howden Ganley lapped their McLaren M10Bs in 56.6s, an average of 117.03mph, Castle Combe instantly became the second fastest national circuit in Britain. Only Silverstone and Thruxton could boast a higher average speed for outright circuit records. Having won the first part convincingly, Gethin

Peter Gethin won the Formula 5000 race on aggregate in May 1970.

Photo: Ferret Fotographics.

was content to spend the second part of the race sitting just behind Ganley, assured of overall victory once the times were added together to produce an aggregate result. The sheer noise and fury of these high-powered single-seaters was enough to leave a lasting impression on all those who witnessed the race, Strawford amongst them. 'That was some of the finest racing I've ever watched or organised,' he says. 'It was lovely to see people like Mike Hailwood doing Formula 5000. To us, that was one of the best meetings of all,' remembers Pat Strawford.

Adding quality to the programme that day was a round of the Lombank Formula 3 Championship, the first time that a major national Formula 3 race had been run at the circuit for more than 15 years. Brazilian star Carlos Pace (Lotus 59) led easily from the start but was slowed by electrical problems and left the way open for David Cole (Lotus 59) to win from Roger Keele (Palliser WDF3) and Pace. Tom Walkinshaw (Lotus 59) was left on the start

line with transmission failure. Completing a memorable day's sport were wins for Colin Vandervell (Merlyn) in Formula Ford, Roy Pierpoint (Rover 3500) in saloons and Alistair Cowin (McLaren M6B) in GTs.

Through the rest of that busy season, many familiar names took race wins including John Turner (Hillman Imp), Shaun Jackson (AC Cobra), Vince Woodman (Ford Escort), Jeremy Lord (Astra RNR), Rhoddy Harvey-Bailey (Ford Falcon), Jonathan Buncombe (BMW 2002), Tony Broster (Dulon LD9B), Tony Shaw (Jaguar E Type) and Brian Cutting (3-litre Martin V8-engined Ford Escort). It had been one of the circuit's best ever seasons in terms of the standard, quantity and quality of racing, but all the time the clock was ticking as the 1971 season approached.

For the motorcycle fans, the season opened on a wet April day for an ACU British Championship meeting. In the 125cc race, Andrew Manship won commandingly but

Swede Ulf Norinder with Mike Hailwood in the Formula 5000 paddock.

Photo: Ferret Fotographics.

Howden Ganley won the second part of the Formula 5000 race in May 1970.

Photo: Ferret Fotographics.

a fierce battle for second was resolved in favour of Barry Sheene at the final corner. His rival Derek Chatterton dropped his bike at Camp and only a fine piece of riding by Sheene avoided a collision as he picked a path between rider and the stricken machine. In July Tony Rutter won twice while the outright circuit record was also beaten when Bryan Kemp (Norton Commando) and Percy Tait (Triumph) both lapped in 1m11.4s (92.77mph). 'Percy Tait was a road tester for the Triumph factory as well as a racer and won a lot of races on 750cc Triumph Triples. You could hear that thing wailing all around the circuit,' recalls Blackman. Sheene,

meanwhile, was in a class of his own in the 125s, with young Rodney Gooch taking third. Much later, Gooch would become a key part of the circuit management team, but back in 1970 he was an ambitious young racer.

'I raced from 1967 on 125s and then 250s, through to 1971,' remembers Gooch. 'At that stage there were two main British championship meetings at Castle Combe and if you were doing the championship you came down here. In 1970 I actually got myself a competitive bike so the excuses went out the window, it was down to the rider. In those days, the Port Talbot club used to try and organise their meetings at Llandow for the Sunday the day after the Castle Combe meetings for those of us coming down from London and the South East. We could belt down the M4, take Barry by storm on Saturday night and race again on Sunday. Then it was the big flog back up what was then only the A4, at 45mph in a Thames van. Castle Combe in those days was very much one of the mainstream circuits and all the stars raced there. The fast circuit was a challenge.

'Barry Sheene was the young upstart then with long hair. I suppose there was a bit of resentment to him initially, but then he showed he really could ride and the resentment very quickly went. His dad Frank was one of

the best two-stroke tuners in the country at the time and they were very close to Bultaco. Barry went on to tremendous things and was a great ambassador for the sport,' says Gooch.

Going into 1971, the safety banks at Quarry in particular were increased in height following the annual RAC circuit inspection. The work was duly completed even though both the temporary planning permission and the MCD sub-lease were due to expire at the end of the season. Sixteen race meetings were scheduled, with three motorcycle meetings and a car calendar again topped by a visit from the European Formula 5000 Championship.

Jeremy Lord and the Astra RNR winning in 1970.

Photo: Trevor Collins.

The extra motorcycle meeting was organised to mark what was expected to be the last year of racing at Castle Combe, even though the financial viability of the meetings was concerning the ACU Wessex Centre. Its Gazette of June 1970 noted that: 'A study of the figures over the past six years showed that attendances had been steadily dropping all the time. We are not in a very satisfactory financial position after the two 1970 events, however we have decided to go ahead with three events in 1971.' The first motorcycle meeting in April brought victories for both Sheene and Rutter before Rutter headed his rival home by two lengths in a cracking 350cc race. Such was their pace that they shared a new circuit record of 1m10.08s, a mark that would stand unchallenged for 10 years before bike racing finally

resumed. Rutter won again in July at the expense of Mick Grant and once more in September as the ACU British Championship meeting brought the curtain down on an unbroken run of 21 seasons.

In March, the car season opened with a BARC meeting notable for a family double as Richard Mallock (Formula Ford) and his elder brother Ray (Clubmans) both won races in front-engined cars produced by the family concern. Ray set a stunning pace in the Clubmans race and set the first 100mph lap for a Clubmans car at what he always considered one of his favourite tracks. Sadly, May 15 dawned wet and stayed that way as the Formula 5000 cars returned to Wiltshire to face pouring rain and a very wet track. Mike Hailwood's return to the

John Burbidge (Jaguar E Type) at Easter 1971.

Photo: Ferret Fotographics.

scene of so many two-wheeled victories was thwarted when his Surtees TS8 blew its engine in unofficial practice on Friday. But in the dry and sunny weather that day, Gethin lapped beneath his own record with a best of 56.2s in Sid Taylor's McLaren M18B.

Due to the soaking track, the race began from a rolling start behind a pace car and turned into a race-long battle between Frank Gardner (Lola T192) and Gethin. Despite repeated attempts to squeeze ahead under braking for Camp, Gethin was destined to take second behind the legendary Australian racer with Ganley taking third after a spin on Farm Straight. The treacherous conditions also claimed the McLaren M7A of Tony Dean which spun down Dean Straight before hitting the marshals' post on the entrance to Camp. Dean was hospitalised with a neck fracture but made a full recovery.

Two heats and a final for the BOC Formula Ford Championship produced plenty of fireworks and marked the Castle Combe debut of South African sensation Jody Scheckter. He got tangled up with John Trevelyan in his heat and it was Jeremy Gambs who won the final in his Lotus 61M after a fierce battle with Dick Barker (Alexis Mk18). Starting well down the grid and hindered by the loss of fourth gear and other drivers' incidents, Scheckter still battled through to fifth in the final.

In fact, Dean was not the only driver hospitalised that day. In practice for the saloon car race Mike Wilds had a major accident in a new Ford Escort. The car hit the marshals' post on the approach to Quarry and Wilds was taken to hospital as a precaution. One of the marshals was also treated on the scene for minor injuries.

In July, the Yellow Pages Formula Atlantic Championship brought more quality single-seater racing from an international field. With Australian Vern Schuppan forced to drive his Palliser on the ignition switch after a throttle return spring broke, Dane Tom Belso was able to sweep ahead in his Brabham BT28/35. When the series returned in August it was Ray Allen (Royale RP8) who headed Schuppan, while the same meeting also featured a round of the Lombank Formula 3 Championship. After heavy rain, Alan Jones (Brabham BT28) won from Colin Vandervell (Brabham BT35) and Scheckter (Merlyn Mk21). Amazingly, two future world

champions shared the Castle Combe podium at the end of that race.

But that was not the last major single-seater action for the season as the Hagley meeting on October 9 was topped by two 10-lap heats and a 30-lap final for the Shell British Formula 3 Championship. Missing from the field was yet another future world champion, however. James Hunt's March 713 was entered but did not arrive. 'On the way to the circuit the tow bar on the team's Ford Galaxie tow car detached itself and the car and trailer hit a lamp post,' explained the Autosport report of the meeting. Scheckter and Roger Williamson won their respective heats while the final kicked off with up to nine cars in a squabbling lead pack.

The early leaders were Scheckter, Williamson and Vandervell, but the latter ran wide and was forced to stop and remove grass and a plastic bag from the nose cone of his Brabham BT35 before his engine temperature reached danger level. The leading group was down to four cars for the final nine laps as Jochen Mass (Brabham BT35) headed Williamson, Scheckter and Rikki von Opel (Lotus 69). 'With two laps to go it was a straight fight between Mass and Scheckter. The German led into Camp for the last time, Scheckter planning to slipstream ahead, but there was a backmarker unwilling to give way. Mass chose exactly the right line to make sure of victory,' said the Motoring News report. After more than 30 minutes of flat-out racing, less than two and a half seconds covered the top four cars as the season, and perhaps the whole Castle Combe history closed on a real high.

In September 1971, John Webb issued a statement announcing that there would be no more motor racing at Castle Combe after the end of October. He referred to: 'The expiry of planning permission for motor racing, practice and related activities, and to local objectors who could become militant if racing were to continue.' However, that statement was quickly countered by AFN. 'The land belongs to Mrs Kitty Thomas and the lease is held by AFN who have no intention of giving up without a fight. Director John Aldington would be looking into the legal position of continuing the circuit's activities next year. MCD had no right to announce that motor racing would stop: their operating rights run out on

October 31,' reported Motoring News on September 16. Strawford was also looking at ways to keep the circuit alive.

'Effectively, the circuit was going to close at the end of 1971. I looked for support from the BRSCC locally and the only support that came forward was to organise a wake for the last meeting. I persuaded them to put in an application for five meetings a year to try and keep the place alive, which they did in February or March 1972. The circuit had closed technically,' says Strawford.

On the back of the previous application to build a new AFN centre and limit racing to just five days, a reprieve was won in June 1972. AFN and Mrs Thomas were granted a further three year temporary planning permission to run five race meetings each year. Although the permission was for three years, it actually covered four seasons as it was due to expire at the end of 1975. At the same time, the RAC required that the earth banks be faced with metal barriers and that new barriers must be constructed along the pit straight. Due to the fact that it was mid-season before planning was granted, only three car events could be arranged in the remaining months of the season with two BRSCC meetings in August and October and a Hagley event in September. Two other planned meetings, one each for the BRSCC and Hagley club, were cancelled from the earlier part of the year.

'The planning permission came through mid-summer but we'd already arranged to run a meeting at Llandow on August Bank Holiday Monday. So we set to, and ran two race meetings on the same day and I drew the short straw and went to Llandow. That was the first meeting of the 'I saved Castle Combe campaign',' recalls Strawford. But before racing could return, considerable work had to be done to build the barriers required by the RAC.

By mid-July the work was progressing well and plans went ahead for the re-opening meeting on August 28. 'The Armco barriers have been ordered and these will be erected by early August. Other work including facing of the bankings has already been done. The RAC has agreed in principle to an increase in the number of starters,' reported the Motoring News of July 13.

To everyone's great relief, the August Bank Holiday Monday meeting went ahead without a hitch and the feature race for Formula Ford was won by American Buzz Buzaglo in the Ippokampos-backed Elden Mk10 from the Royale RP3 of Bristolian Roger Orgee. John Turner (Ford Anglia) and Terry Sanger (Chevrolet Camaro) won saloon car races while a round of the Ford Escort Mexico series was won by Andy Rouse. After the Hagley club meeting, the three-meeting season concluded with another BRSCC meeting in October when notable winners were Vince Woodman (Ford Escort), John Sheldon (Lotus 69F) and Ray Mallock (Mallock U2 Mk11).

'The initial plan was that the five days would be split up into two days for the BRSCC, one for the BARC, one for the Hagley club and one for the Wessex centre of the ACU. We all had a meeting at Mrs Thomas' house and John Aldington put it to us that the company could not survive on five days a year. He said the rent would have to go up. Much to my delight, a man called Vic Anstice from the local centre of the ACU, made a speech based on the fact that Castle Combe had been too expensive to hire for years and they had come to the meeting looking for a decrease. So I said, I'll have his date if he doesn't want it!' recalls Strawford. That move would mean that motorcycle racing would be absent from Castle Combe for nine years.

However, for the 1973 season only, the fifth date was taken over by the Aston Martin Owners' Club. After a couple of smaller meetings, the 1973 season was topped by the BRSCC's Fordsport Day on June 16, when the action centred on Ford-powered categories as well as a celebrity race for race and rally drivers in standard Ford Consul GTs. On reflection, it was always likely to end in disaster and it proved to be an expensive event for Ford.

Press reports recall the drama and ultimate carnage for which the race is best remembered. 'Coming around Camp Roger Clark and David Brodie were lurching in with lots of understeer, promoted to vicious oversteer at the apex by either taking to the grass or being sheer bloody-minded by keeping the throttle hard down.' By lap six the order was Brodie, Richard Longman, Roger Clark, Tony Pond, Andy Rouse and Tony Fall. 'Going up

David Da Costa's Escort Mexico on the grid.

Photo: Julian Hann.

towards the marshals' post on the inside towards Quarry, Pond and Longman were trying for the same line over the bump. Longman went sideways into the marshals' post, dislodging earth, sleepers, Armco and supports, while Pond came into the side of him,' reported Autosport. Rouse won the race which was stopped after eight laps, two laps short. 'Despite his seat being no more than 18 inches wide, Longman escaped with a broken pelvis,' said Autosport. Only three cars finished the race without dents and marshal Robin Mansfield was also taken to hospital along with Longman.

Terry Fisher (Merlyn Mk20A) led the main Formula Ford race until his engine expired on the eighth lap, leaving Don Macleod to win in the early Van Diemen. 1973 was the first season for the fledgling constructor and the FA73 chassis that Macloed raced that day was the

initial design from Ralph Firman's company. A Ford Sports race for GT40s and AC Cobras was won by Paul Weldon's GT40 while the Escort Mexico race went to Devon racer David Da Costa. Escorts also dominated the special saloons race that featured a three car dice between Andy Rouse (Broadspeed Escort BDA), Brian Cutting (Escort Martin V8) and John Turner (Escort BRM V8). Rouse spun and Cutting retired once more, leaving Turner to win.

In August, the BARC took over with a range of national championships including Formula 3 and Formula Ford. Ian Taylor (March 733) won what seems likely to have been the last ever contemporary championship Formula 3 race at the circuit while rising star Stephen South (Ray 73F) won the Wella for Men Formula Ford race. Richard Lloyd (Chevrolet Camaro)

Richard Longman turns into Quarry in 1974.

Photo: John Gaisford.

beat Gordon Spice (Ford Capri) to win the Production Saloon race and Jeremy Lord (Lola T212) was the best of the Motoring News GT Championship field.

A wonderful array of classic and historic cars gathered in September for the Aston Martin Owners' Club meeting when the Daily Mirror Historic Car race was won by Peter Waller (ERA B-Type). Charles Lucas was also a winner in Hesketh Racing's Maserati Birdcage and he added another win in a Ferrari 275LM despite starting

from the back of the grid. Also a double winner was Michael Salmon in the rare Aston Martin Project 212 as the 1973 season concluded in style.

In 1974 another five-meeting programme was put together with three for the BRSCC, one for the BARC and one for the Hagley club. However, the BRSCC's July 13 meeting was greatly enhanced by the arrival of the competitors in the Avon Tour of Britain. In April, the season opened with a thrilling Formula Ford race won by

Roger Orgee after a fine battle with Bryan Sharp and Ian Moore. A young Jeff Allam raced his Vauxhall Viva GT to third in the special saloon race, finishing behind Bryan Cutting and Terry Sanger. A month later the Hagley meeting celebrated 50 years of the Frazer Nash marque.

But it was the July meeting that marked the highlight of the season as four races for the Tour of Britain competitors followed on from a traditional race meeting. The Avon-backed tour was for production saloons competing over a series of races and tarmac special stages around the south of England. With backing from locally-based Avon Tyres, it was fitting that its visit to Castle Combe represented the final race meeting of the 1974 event. Grand Prix stars James Hunt and Jody Scheckter both retired from the tour before the cars arrived at Castle Combe and the event was being dominated by the works-entered Ford Escort RS2000s of Roger Clark and Gerry Marshall. Their sideways antics won the hearts of the crowds that year and in another door-handling battle at Castle Combe, Clark won by a whisker from Marshall. Other races for the tour competitors brought wins for Tony Lanfranchi (BMW CSL), Andrew Cowan (Vauxhall Magnum) and Bernard Unett (Hillman Avenger).

Two meetings in August concluded the season with leading racers including Phil Winter (Mini), Creighton Brown (Mallock U2), Mick Hill (Special Saloon Ford Capri), Syd Fox (Formula Ford Hawke DL11) and John Turner (Special Saloon Skoda-Chevrolet). However, even as the 1974 season wound up, thoughts were once again turning to the future of the circuit, for probable closure once again loomed at the end of the 1975 season.

Howard Strawford was about to take a pivotal role in the fight to keep the circuit open. 'I had recently given the general manager at Kraft Foods the benefit of my opinion. He invited me to London to discuss it and sacked me on the spot, which just proved that he was a fool! The only good thing was that I got a job on the train coming back home. That was just as well as I was a penniless organiser at the time. I managed to get a job with a French company selling fruit which was one of the best things that ever happened to me. It went very well but then they started getting nervous that I would leave.

They said, 'take a breath, Howard. We don't mind as long as you keep the business.

'One day in 1975 Mrs Thomas rang me out of the blue and said: 'You're definitely interested in trying to look after the future of the circuit, aren't you?' We met a couple of hours later and she said, 'I want you to take on running the circuit.' By co-incidence at this stage, I was a trainer of stewards for the RAC and by chance that weekend I was training Welsh accountant Robert Davies. So, within a matter of days a consortium was made up with him as financial advisor, Philip Boobyer and myself. I thought if we were going to pull it off we needed the BRSCC involved so I offered the club a stake in the circuit. We formed a company and opened a bank account and I was very grateful for Bob's expertise in that area,' recalls Strawford.

'We went to a meeting in London where AFN effectively told me that if we wanted to run the sport there until it went bankrupt, that was okay by them. They were glad to get out of it. We agreed a price which was significant but wouldn't meet the cost of a Ford Escort today. That was for the company and its assets, the fixtures and fittings and then we negotiated a new lease with Mrs Thomas. In fairness, AFN said they would not take money off us until the planning permission was renewed.

'I first had a warning directly from John Aldington when we were buying the company that I might manage to get three or four years' sport out of the company, but I would never get the planning situation changed. It would simply be a case of running it until the RAC insisted we spend money on it or something of that sort, and that would be it. When the lease was renewed I went along for the signing at the solicitors, the rather aged Mr Forrester got all the papers out. He sat opposite me and said: 'I have to ask you a question. Do you really know what you're taking on?' Well I said "yes", but the real answer was probably "no". But my view on it was that I'd been a very successful salesman for many years and I was convinced I could sell my way out of the troubles. In the fullness of time that turned out to be right.

'When we set up the company, I was considered to be quite mad by some potential investors. I approached two

Brian Prebble's Hillman Imp heads a 1974 saloon pack.

Photo: John Gaisford.

well-known West Country drivers, who shall remain nameless, and asked them for £1000 investment. They both turned me down laughing, thinking I was mad getting involved with a company that was going to go under. I do occasionally remind them of that,' adds Strawford with a grin.

It was undoubtedly a tough time for the Strawfords. 'When Mrs Thomas asked him to take over the lease, that was a big gamble. Bob Davies was a key part of it, especially in the early days and encouraged Howard. Philip Boobyer was very supportive as well,' says Pat Strawford.

'We set about getting the planning renewed and in 1975 I effectively ran it for six months without people realising we'd taken it over. It wasn't until the planning came through that we finalised the deal. The only person working on the circuit was Bill Little who used to live in Westway Farm. There was an old Mk1 Land Rover, a 1949 Porsche tractor and a rare scooter. I advertised the tractor and the scooter in the BRSCC magazine, British Racing News. Would you believe, it started a Dutch auction. I thought £100 would have been okay but we ended up getting about £750. Which did no harm at all,' says Strawford. Fortunately, he had taken out several insurance premiums when he started work and they all matured in the lead up to the purchase of the circuit. 'I literally bought the place for twelve shillings and six pence a week,' he says.

While these negotiations progressed, the 1975 season was running along with five meetings. In truth, it was a pretty low-key season although special saloon races and the local Formula Ford series provided some good racing. In saloons, leading contenders included Mini racers John Coundley and John Routley, Brian Cutting (now with an Oldsmobile V8 engine in his Ford Escort), Chris Simms (Vauxhall Viva), Brian Prebble (Hillman Imp) and John Morgan (Jaguar). In June the fresh-faced 17 year-old Ian Flux won a Formula Vee race in his first season of racing, while in September former Superstox World Champion Derek Warwick finished second in a Formula Ford heat in his Hawke DL12.

Strawford was under no illusion about the precarious financial situation that the circuit faced. 'It didn't take a master brain to work out that the company wasn't going to survive on five meetings a year. So I went for a meeting with Wiltshire County Council to ascertain what could be done. It was like walking into a deep freeze. I had a totally and utterly worthless meeting when they explained that we couldn't do anything but cut the grass and maintain the site on the other 360 days a year. We needed planning permission for everything.

'The planning officer was exceptionally civil once he realised I didn't have the faintest clue what I was talking about. He took me out in the corridor and said: 'It's not for me to advise you, but you desperately need a planning consultant.' He gave me three names and by a strange co-incidence Clive Power was my dentist and was also racing here in Formula Fords. I'd been to a party at his house in Corsham a couple of months before and I'd met one of these blokes, and that was Martin Chick.

'I rang him up and he was fully qualified and had worked for Wiltshire County Council. But he'd left, would you believe, because he didn't like the holidays. One of his hobbies was offshore yacht crewing. We met and I decided I didn't need to look any further. As a result of that, we started an association that continued for 25

years. We adopted a policy of slowly, slowly, and I went off to investigate things we might ask for that were suitably innocuous,' says Strawford.

The most pressing problem was to gain an extension to the planning permission that was going to expire on December 31 1975. Encouragingly this was finally granted for a further five years, taking it until the end of 1980, and permission was also granted for a number of days testing for fully silenced cars. However, the process was not quite complete when the time came for the opening meeting of the season on Easter Monday. Various challenges were made about the circuit hosting a race meeting, but no action was taken and the event went ahead as planned.

'Under the guidance of Bob Davies, AFN (Castle Combe) Ltd was acquired from Porsche and its name changed to Castle Combe Circuit Ltd. I set two objectives, one short-term to make the company viable, which was too obvious for words. This was largely achieved by a calculation on the back of a fag packet that showed no one was paying enough. Then I set a long term aim to get the usage up to the level of Thruxton, which was 12 race days and 90 quiet days a year. This was quite ambitious as we only had five days a year and so an increase to 102 was a big step. It was ambitious and it took 10 years, but we did achieve it. A new lease was granted by Mrs Thomas and when this was all in place the take-over was announced in August 1976,' says Strawford.

The first meeting to be held under the ownership of Castle Combe Circuit Ltd was on September 11 1976. Already, he had identified the need to greatly expand circuit activities and a Motoring News report in April 1976 showed just how pressing a need this really was. 'Last year the net revenue was only £6000 and this was insufficient to cover costs, so wider use is clearly necessary to make the track viable,' said the story.

The 1976 programme comprised five car meetings, three for the BRSCC, one for the Hagley club and one for the BARC. Additionally, the Texaco Tour of Britain visited the circuit on July 10 for four 12-lap races with an entry that included former Formula 1 World Champion

Denny Hulme (Opel Commodore) and future World Rally Champion Ari Vatanen (Ford Escort RS2000). Importantly, this would be the final season for clubs other than the BRSCC running meetings at the circuit.

'I realised that the circuit hire terms were far too generous for the clubs, who had always done very well at Castle Combe, particularly on the Bank Holidays. All of the organisers shared the gate receipts equally with the circuit. I think the circuit hire rate at the time was £600. I'd been used to running hillclimbs in South Wales and

'I also ran a time and motion study on the whole enterprise, although I didn't realise what it was at the time. Because I'd been involved for seven years, I could see what was wrong with it. When you go to a race meeting as a steward, you witness all sorts of ridiculous things going on, not the least of which is the reasons clubs give for not being able to start on time. The number one favourite was that the doctors weren't there. Peter Baskett was a regular visitor and I stitched the poor chap up there and then,' recalls Strawford of the appointment of the circuit's chief medical officer.

The marshals tend to an errant Formula Ford driver.

you could pay that much to rent a hillclimb venue. So the first thing I had to do was say sorry to Hagley and the BARC and change the terms around so that the circuit, advertised and promoted the meetings and collected all the gate revenue. At the same time, I raised the track hire fee considerably. As Competition Secretary of the South Western Centre I could see both sides of the finances and knew that the club would continue to make money. The circuit had to make some money to survive.

'The best way to address problems like these was to get rid of the other clubs and do it ourselves. I soon realised one of the key things was to have the catering open before the meeting started. When we took over, the caterer was a health risk to the county so he went. We used another caterer for a couple of years but then we set up Tavern Catering and the rule was that it was open from 7am. As a result of starting on time, we were able to fit in more races. The crowds loved it.

Nigel Mansell (Hawke DL11) in one of his early races at Castle Combe.

Photo: John Gaisford.

'As Clerk of the Course, I was very aware of the delays in getting cars out onto the grid. So I came up with the idea of gridding the cars while the winners of the previous race were being interviewed in front of the grid, and while the breakdown vehicles were clearing the track. We soon saved five minutes on each race and were able to run 11 or even 12 races in a day and gross even more income for the club. This was eventually copied a lot and went on to become the basis for the Racing Ahead method of running race meetings,' recalls Strawford.

The 1976 season started in April with a BRSCC meeting notable for several star names in the entry list. Having a bit of fun in Bill Stone's Classic Saloon Morris Minor was race car constructor Adrian Reynard while trainee doctor Jonathan Palmer won the Modified Sports Car race in his 3-litre Marcos. In July, the Dunlop Star of Tomorrow Formula Ford 1600 brought a crop of young hopefuls to the circuit and the opening heat was won by an ambitious former karter from Birmingham called Nigel Mansell. In September, during a cracking 10-race meeting, Mansell won again.

It was a case of more of the same for the 1977 season, but now all five meetings would be run by the South Western Centre of the BRSCC. It was to be a year of consolidation for the new owners, but already the ground work was being done in readiness for another attack on the planning situation. Improvements in facilities were noted when the season opened on Easter Monday during a meeting notable for the lengths that Vince Woodman went to in his bid to win at two circuits on one day. Having won a round of the British Touring Car Championship at Thruxton in a Group One Ford Capri, Woodman flew to Castle Combe in time to win the Special Saloon race in his glorious 3.4-litre Cologne Capri. Although the engine started to go sick later in the race, Woodman still finished well clear of the Vauxhall Firenza of Geoff Janes. The season ended with another Woodman victory in October while John Bowtell (March 74B) saw off Roger Orgee (Elden Mk18) for Formula Libre victory in the final race of the season.

'At that time, the RAC insisted that the promises that had gone on for many years about updating the safety system had to be delivered. Robert Langford of the RAC took a fairly firm line as we were new owners. As such we were expected to start with a clean sheet of paper. At the time, armco cost £33 for a three-metre length, without nuts and bolts. So a double row with posts would cost around £100 for three metres and I was looking for two miles of it. So I started to investigate the second-hand market even though no one in this country had used second-hand. I was still travelling the country for the French company at this stage and I started calling into motorway repair depots.

'I discovered they were exceedingly wasteful with what they did with it. They piled the damaged stuff in a corner and when the pile got too big, they called in the scrap man. Because of the spindly supports they used on the motorways, an accident might only damage two sections, but knock over 10 sections. So there was no point in selling it to a scrap man if eight of the sections were undamaged. I started offering twice what the scrap

man was offering. We had some good friends in the area and the chap who owned Castle Combe Dairies said that any afternoon I wanted a lorry I could use his. Les Rawlings, from our rescue unit, drove for him at the dairy, so he would travel around the West Country picking up as many as 80 sheets of armco at a time. I soon started to make a bit of an art form out of buying and selling this stuff. Eventually, Alan Wilson, the circuits director for Brands Hatch, rang me up and asked me if I could supply them! So I just re-directed some of the lorries and adjusted the prices accordingly. The amusing thing was that the stuff I sold to Brands Hatch came from the motorway by the side of the circuit,' says Strawford.

All of this trading was all done through the company and was quite a boost to the finances of Castle Combe Circuit Ltd. None of those involved were taking any expenses and so any profit made was ploughed straight back into the circuit.

Nigel Mansell (43) takes an outside line at Quarry during a Formula Ford race.

Photo: John Gaisford.

A Mini gets into trouble at Old Paddock.

'Quite by chance, not long after we bought the company, Llandow was to close in financial disaster. Unbeknown to most people the South Wales Automobile Club, the owners of Llandow, had bought all the surplus armco that was taken down when the M1 was widened. There were thousands and thousands of sheets. The circuit closed in a big hurry and I did a deal with them to buy it all, complete with wooden posts and bolts. It was somewhere between 12 and 20 lorry loads. At the time, one of my fellow directors was Philip Boobyer who worked for Tower Scaffolding and helped enormously with the transportation. Another very good friend of mine was the late Barry Reece who was general manager for Greenham Plant and their low-loaders carried a lot of armco.

'We went over on a Sunday morning with two lorries from each company and two working parties, one made up of volunteers from the club and one of agricultural workers from around Castle Combe. We moved it over

here and started installing barriers at the approach to Tower with the intention of going down to the startline. The plan was to re-open Tower to spectators by putting in half a mile of armco over the winter,' says Strawford.

Construction of the new barriers required a huge amount of work over the winter of 1977/78 and an army of willing volunteers played a vital part in getting the work done. Notable members of the working party included the circuit's long standing chief medical officer Peter Baskett, Roy Hancock, Philip Boobyer, Ted Reece, Tiny Greenhill and Bob McInnes, chief of the circuit's rescue vehicle at the time. 'I had to ban going to the pub at lunch time otherwise we'd only get a couple of hours' work done on a Sunday morning. But I organised refreshments instead,' recalls Strawford.

The benefit of their efforts was apparent as the 1978 season started. Spectator access was now available from Camp all the way to the exit of Quarry, allowing fans to watch at Avon Rise for the first time since the early 1950s. Extensive landscaping provided a raised earth bank in front of the old quarry to further improve viewing, while the Quarry marshals' post was also moved from the position where it was hit by Richard Longman in 1973. This work also allowed the enlargement of the Chippenham Road car park and offered spectator viewing around more than a mile and a quarter of the track. With the approval of the RAC, the number of starters permitted was increased to 28 in time for the May Bank Holiday meeting.

'We kept upgrading the safety system and I compared our grid size with Llandow, which had also been 20 on only a one-mile circuit. With every safety upgrade, we pursued the RAC to lift the grid size and soon it was up 50% to 30 cars. These changes all worked and we were able to increase the rent accordingly because the club was able to run more races with more cars in each of them. As the BRSCC was a share-holder in the circuit, it had knowledge of the financial restrictions we were working under and fully understood the situation,' says Strawford.

Leading names to race at the circuit in 1978 included future grand prix racer Kenny Acheson who won a Townsend Thoresen Formula Ford race in July in his Royale RP24 and South African lady Desiree Wilson who won the Formula Ford 2000 race at the same meeting. But it was the off-track activity that was most significant that year as Strawford and Chick prepared to go back to the planning authorities. Adding weight to their efforts were new silencing rules set to be imposed by the RAC for the 1979 season that would reduce the overall noise levels generated by many club racing categories.

'With Martin Chick looking after our planning applications, we started adding little activities like HGV driver training, tyre testing and a few dealer demonstration days. We got temporary planning permission for all these activities and things like cycling. Eventually we got a bit braver and we decided to try setting up a racing school. When I took over, I discovered a letter on file from Mike Knight wanting to come and set up a school for his company *Ecole de Pilotage Winfield*.

We tried for temporary planning for two years and they refused it. So Martin said it was time for an appeal.

'When we did the first public enquiry into permanent permission, it was still very much the blind leading the blind. In particular, I did two things that were useful. I managed to lobby an awful lot of people to write letters of support. Secondly, our trees suffered very badly from Dutch elm disease and you could see the racing from the main road at Quarry. So I found a landscaping company and we managed to get a Countryside Commission grant and did a major landscaping programme in the late 1970s.

'We also closed the footpath through the woods behind Quarry and built a raised bank in front of the wood. I approached Wiltshire County Council about building a tip on the outside of Quarry and they agreed to build this tip for me at no cost. They then cleared out an old depot that they had which was full of old paving stones and kerb stones. They topped it off and we had the spectator bank at Quarry. Needless to say, I confirmed this in writing with them and they confirmed back that they were doing the work.

'When we went to the public enquiry I was cross examined about having built these banks illegally. Well, as it happened, part of my presentation folder was copies of these letters! You couldn't have the council suing us for tipping things illegally when it was them doing it,' recalls Strawford.

'At the start of the day of public enquiries you had to submit your name and address if you wished to speak during the enquiry, and about 15 or 20 people did this. Among them was a man from the Countryside Commission and he was obviously very anti motor racing. But included in my presentation was this landscaping programme which had been paid for by the Countryside Commission and administered by Wiltshire County Council. Funnily enough, this chap didn't come back after lunch.

'They decided not to give us a decision on the cycle racing which was incredibly good luck and it was such a stupid thing for them to have done. I was able to make contact with the Sports Minister of the time, Hector Munro. I was doing all my own lobbying and PR and I rang up the regional director for the Sports Council. By good chance it was the first time the Sports Council was trying to get some private land for cycle racing because it was seen to be a bit dangerous on public roads. That led to the Minister for Sport intervening at the Department of Town and Country Planning and making some lovely waves. The Sports Council paid the rent for the first year to get cycle racing off the ground. We charged something like £25 a day. We've carried on having cycle racing right through to the present day and we run as many as 18 cycle race meetings each year,' says Strawford.

The net result was that temporary planning permission was granted for a two-year period for heavy goods vehicle testing, automobile tyre testing and dealer demonstration days, but planning was refused for the racing school. Other improvements continued to be made and by March 1979, barriers had been installed from Dean Straight to Camp, while the high earth bank had been removed to improve spectator viewing. The pit signalling area was improved and a cantilevered starters' rostrum constructed. An automatic red light race stopping system was installed thanks to a donation from the Phil Winter Memorial Fund. Phil had been a marshal and then competitor at Castle Combe in a very quick special saloon Mini before being the innocent victim of a tragic road accident on the Isle of Man while spectating at the 1977 TT motorcycle races.

Refusal of permission for the racing school led Strawford and Chick into a second appeal and another public enquiry. 'Martin had read about a public enquiry that he was impressed with where the solicitor had used a barrister from Bristol called Donald Hawkins who, by chance, also happened to be the Bristol coroner. He impressed Martin and he certainly impressed me. When we went to the public enquiry the best way to describe him was like a Shakespearean actor. He had various ploys and the best one was that he wore a pair of half-rimmed glasses on a gold chain. He could put these on and off as though he was on the stage at Stratford on Avon and he could make such a big issue of it. He was a stunning performer. He was 6ft 3 with a back like a guardsman and beautifully spoken,' recalls Strawford.

'We realised at this stage that noise was a bit of a problem and rather cheekily I used Roy Hancock from the BRSCC South Western centre as a DIY noise expert. He is a consultant physicist by profession with some very impressive qualifications. I was quite astonished that while I was being cross-examined by Wiltshire County Council they started asking me what I thought would be a fair level of usage for the circuit. It completely flummoxed me and I had to be guided by Hawkins to go on and answer the question. We'd gone to talk about racing schools and I wondered what the hell that had to do with it.

'I pondered for a couple of minutes and thought that the best thing I could say was the level of usage they had at Thruxton. I said what I would regard as a fair deal would be a dozen days of motor racing and quite a lot of days of silent activity, which might include a racing school. 25 years later, that was where we had got to!' says Strawford.

'Mike Knight came to the enquiry but was desperately put off by it. Previously, on Martin Chick's advice, we had laid on a demonstration of what a racing school would be like. Before the demonstration, we gathered the assembled masses, which needless to say were all objectors, and spoke to them. The hostility was incredible. We held the meeting in the building that Merlin occupies now and we moved a car there. I stood on a stage and talked, then demonstrated the car and how quiet it was with secondary silencers fitted. There were a group of objectors mouthing off and Mike was not keen on that.

'We ended up taking 18 months to get a two-year temporary permission that would expire in six months. It was hardly surprising that Mike didn't want to start and so I came up with the idea of using it for training. Instead of Castle Combe Racing School, we started running training days and practice days with an element of tuition. We were then encouraged to pursue this negotiated plan for a fair deal. It had to go to three committees at that stage and when it got to the last committee it was turned down,' explains Strawford.

And so the battle lines were drawn for yet another appeal as the decade came to a conclusion. Having seemed doomed to close earlier in the 1970s, the circuit had survived largely due to the unfailing efforts of Strawford and his small team. The five-year planning permission granted back in 1975 was due to expire at the end of 1980 but the slowly, slowly policy was starting to reap dividends as the range and number of circuit activities increased. Strawford was now preparing to go on the offensive once more.

Chapter 7

The 1980s

-

permanent planning at last

In March 1980 following the latest public enquiry, permission for the racing school was finally given by the Minister for the Environment, Michael Heseltine. It led to the immediate creation of the Castle Combe Racing School with Mike Knight initially involved as manager for the venture. The concept was for a series of one-day sessions for owners of FF1600 cars with fully-silenced engines. Early instructors included Gareth Lloyd, Ian Moore and Mike Taylor.

While the planning battles continued, the 1980 season was in full swing, but it was a year tinged with tragedy. In April, regular Castle Combe racer Chris Inch suffered a heart attack during practice. His Mini 1275GT came to a halt on the infield without any damage, but poor Inch was dead. In May, Hillman Imp racer Wendy Wathen crashed heavily and died a week later in hospital.

On a happier note, that same meeting featured a round of the Formula Atlantic Championship won by David Leslie and a round of the BMW County Challenge that pitted star drivers into battle in a group of identical 323i BMWs in standard trim. Winner of that race was a young Martin Brundle who also finished second in the Formula Ford 2000 race.

Having been encouraged during the previous enquiry to pursue a negotiated plan for a 'fair deal' settlement, Strawford and Chick went back to the planning authorities once more in the spring of 1980. The proposals sought permanent planning permission, including 12 race days rather than five plus four practice days on weekdays, but a reduction in racing school days

from 60 to 20 days. Additionally, their application pledged a programme of environmental improvements, including better toilet facilities, further tree screens and more noise limiting banks. The package fell in line with government policy of the day regarding employment, recreation, use of existing facilities and reducing spending by local government. In making the application, Castle Combe Circuit Ltd proposed that the granting of permanent planning permission would save the local councils considerable time and money in the future.

'We had now moved into the time of Mrs Thatcher, who I must say was very good for us. Particularly as she set up Michael Heseltine to carry out a review of local government as Secretary of State. Through that came the local government re-organisation and the birth of the North Wilts. District Council. This didn't happen overnight, of course. And the Government also brought out policies against unemployment in the countryside, leisure activities in the countryside and specifically, directives aimed at the multiple usage of existing facilities,' recalls Strawford.

'The number of small usages we'd got at the time included the racing school which was 60 days a year and they didn't like that. The deal that evolved was to increase the number of race days from five to 12 and reduce the racing school from 60 to 20. That would give them an overall reduction from 65 days to 32. It seemed to me to be an excellent idea, and it brought us to public enquiry number three,' says Strawford.

In September 1980 the proposals were rejected by Wiltshire County Council, despite being approved by two parish councils and the District Council and gaining support from 333 local residents through a petition while just 15 were against the circuit's plans. 'So that led to public inquiry number three, which was for 12 days motor racing,' says Strawford. The appeal against this latest decision was to be made to the Department of the Environment and would, inevitably, lead to another public inquiry.

Remarkably, the County Council had encouraged the application for permanent planning in the first place, only to turn it down. It seems as though the Council's decision may have been influenced by a group of objectors known as the Yatton Keynell and Castle Combe Environmental Council. Its aims were: 'The preservation and protection of the local environment, with special reference to the control of motor racing and allied pursuits.'

A leading objector against the circuit was Major Peter Phillips, father of Captain Mark Phillips. At the time he was quoted in the local press: 'If you accept this, in a very short time ways and means would be found to use the circuit for one use or another every day of the year.' Protestors claimed that permanent planning permission could lead to crowds of leather-coated motorcyclists converging on Castle Combe from Bristol to the Midlands. Seemingly influenced by this group, the County Council rejected the application for permanent planning and advised that a less ambitious proposal should be put forward. The choices for the circuit were to submit a revised proposal or appeal the decision at a public inquiry. Strawford and Chick readily opted for the inquiry.

'Donald Hawkins decided we needed an expert witness. 'Moss, Hunt or Stewart will do,' he said. 'We didn't have £1500 to our name and they were going to want a lot more than that. By a strange co-incidence I was a little involved with Nick Brittain. Through Bob Davies I'd ended up running the first rallysprint in the country, if not the world, at Esgair Dafydd. I was clerk of the course for the event and Nick promoted it. Nick knew all these people of course, so he said he'd arrange it for us,' recalls Strawford.

'Moss would have loved to have done it but he was already committed somewhere else. Stewart was available but we couldn't afford him. So Nick Brittain rang James Hunt and we did a deal with him. I have to say that James won me over in the biggest possible way and I became an enormous fan of his. Because we could only have him for one day, we had a couple of things to sort out, not least was that Nick had told him he had to wear a suit and a tie. So I wrote to him and confirmed this but my mistake was that I didn't mention shoes. He had a famous pair of trainers that he wore for about 10 years. So we had the suit and the tie, but with the trainers.

'We arranged a breakfast meeting at the Old Bell at Sutton Benger. I went along with Martin Chick and Hunt arrived in his suit, tie and trainers driving a monster left-hooker Mercedes. He won over Hawkins in a matter of minutes. He was such a smoothie, it wasn't true. I'd organised a photo shoot and I had both regional BBC and ITV coming down. As we headed for the door, Hawkins said to Hunt, 'You're a true blue British lad who has done very well, but you're not driving that bloody Mercedes! You'll go with Howard in his old Range Rover.'

'So he parked the Mercedes up and jumped in with me and we drove into Chippenham. There were two or three surprises during the day but the biggest of all was how good James was. I stopped outside the council offices and because it was a public inquiry there was no parking. He got out and immediately had all the TV and cameras in front of him and he was making wonderful comments like: 'Where would this country be without grass roots racing circuits like Castle Combe. People like me would have no opportunity to go forward!' He was wonderful,' says Strawford.

'When he finally finished this long answer to a question about racing schools and about training, the chap from the BBC said to him: 'Would you want to live in Castle Combe next to the circuit?' Hunt replied: 'Young man, do you live next door to the BBC in Whiteladies Road in Bristol? It would be more convenient, wouldn't it? Too much traffic, too much coming and going for you?' The BBC guy was totally gobsmacked! We hadn't even got into the door of the public inquiry.

'The good bit very, very soon back-fired on us. Unbeknown to me, Mrs Thomas had decided that she was coming to the public inquiry. She was a dear lady who I got on with terribly well, but she could be crude. We said our pieces and it appeared to have gone well. On the list of speakers was Mr Payne, head of the objectors. The things he could think of to say about us were incredible. He had statistics and little note books and it only took about five minutes for Mrs Thomas to call out 'liar!' She was on the front benches with us and continued to interrupt. The inspector soon tired of this and told Hawkins to control his people. Hawkins turned to Hunt, who was sitting behind him, and said: 'I hear you're good with women, deal with her!' So he got up out of his seat and walked into the next tier to sit next to Mrs Thomas. He whispered in her ear for about a minute, put his hand on her knee and she cooed like a bird until lunchtime. It was brilliant,' remembers Strawford.

'It was after this third public enquiry that we actually won permanent planning permission, albeit we only got eight days for racing. The 12 days got cut to eight and it had taken us thirty years to achieve it and had cost us, I estimate, £25,000 in legal charges and professional fees. Thirty years earlier they could have bought a certificate of established usage for five shillings. But I suppose if they had, they'd have made a success of the circuit and I wouldn't have been able to buy it!'

The public inquiry had been held in late February and, of course, the temporary planning permission had expired at the end of 1980. However, in order that the 1981 five-meeting programme could proceed, a further temporary permission was granted until June 1980 while the deliberations of the inspector were awaited. When finally announced, the inspector's verdict also recommended that the matter should be reviewed in two years to consider an increase from eight to 10 days racing.

'Castle Combe saved,' ran the Autosport headline. National editor Marcus Pye reported that the battle to save the circuit was finally over and, 31 years into its history, the circuit finally had permanent planning permission. The news was received with delight and relief throughout the sport after Strawford's 10-year

battle to get permanent permission for racing and other activity on the circuit.

'The decision came at the end of June 1981 and it wasn't terribly easy to organise more meetings at that stage of the season. We'd only planned to run five meetings, but if we managed to run eight it would bring a significant upturn in our income. That brought the return of motorcycle racing to Castle Combe. We invited North Gloucester Motor Cycle Club to run a race meeting and we ran one extra meeting ourselves. The final day was used for a sprint run by Welsh Counties Car Club,' says Strawford. Both extra race meetings were squeezed in during October.

'We put together 30 days per annum of activities that were totally innocuous and applied for them for a temporary period only. Martin Chick's plan was quite simple. The planners could not refuse permission without having experience of the usage. So we let them monitor the days and made sure they found nothing to complain about. The activities were tyre testing, originally by Avon Tyres, HGV training and dealer days. Activity number four was an absolute stunner. Agricultural dead stock sales fitted in very well with the rural image and turned out to give us some of the best planning permission we've ever got. Dead stock sales are classified in the same way as a Sunday market in planning law. The other activity was caravan rallies, which don't need planning as the major caravan organisations hold exemption certificates. The trials of all these activities went very well and gave North Wiltshire District Council no reason not to renew the planning. We also obtained very useful planning permission to run a steam rally. I say it was very useful because it was a weekend event and was one of the first things ever to be held at Castle Combe on a Sunday.

'The only reason I started running car boot sales was because of Mike Knight. He said: 'You should run car boot sales. You could do a lot for the locals and it would be good PR.' But I used to tell him to shut up and stop going on about it. In the end, he told me there was this massive car boot sale up at Ascot and I should go up and see it. Eventually he invited us all up there for Sunday lunch. When we were driving down the road following his map, I realised we were driving past a car boot sale.

So he took us down to see it and it was enlightening because they had this great big sign outside like a thermometer showing how much had been raised for charity that year.' The whole concept of car boot sales would become an important feature of Castle Combe's activities in the coming years.

'I never liked the idea, but to cut a long story short we got planning permission. I decided that if we were going to diversify, we should do it properly and we now run the biggest car boot sale in the West Country. We regularly fill the paddock completely with sellers and have had over 500 sellers. The car parks are often full and we bring people in by bus to the paddock. It is 25p to come in and we have, for many years, given the gate proceeds to local charities. In 1998 alone, more than £14,000 was raised for local charities,' says Strawford.

The increase in race days opened up the chance for the return of motorcycle racing after a nine-year absence and Strawford invited the North Glos Motor Cycle Club to run what would become an annual event. The return to Castle Combe was greeted with enthusiasm by the motorcycle racing fraternity, but the local residents were less keen. Their fears were to prove totally unfounded, but it did provide Strawford with one of his favourite tales.

'When we got the increase to eight days of racing I got the North Gloucester club to organise a motor bike meeting, even though the locals weren't happy about having motorbikers rampaging around. Because I wasn't acting as Clerk of the Course, I didn't have much to do on the day, so I decided I'd drive quietly around the area in the morning to see what impact the motorbike fans were having. It was a load of fuss about nothing. I drove around for two hours, stopping here and there and there was nothing to see. People were quietly going about their business. Eventually I drove down into Castle Combe village and sat out in the square with a glass of lager. I couldn't hear or see anything so I went back to the office.

'I sat down and the phone rang. It was the landlady of the White Hart pub in the village. 'I thought you'd like to know there are motorcyclists rampaging through the village.' I said: 'Come off it, I've just come back from there.' She said: 'As I talk to you, there are motorcyclists

going through the village swinging chains around.' I said; 'Sit where you are, I'm coming back.' So I shot back down in the car and I found the two motorcyclists clad in black leather. They were swinging a chain around, they were looking for someone to help repair it because it had snapped! They must have been nearly 70 years old. They'd got this old Norton out to come to the circuit and the chain had broken. I just creased up!'

That first meeting for the return of motorcycle racing was eagerly awaited by many, including Andy Blackman. 'When motorcycle racing returned, I put up a £100 prize for the person who could break one of the old lap records by the greatest margin. That went to Mick Boddice with his sidecar,' he recalls. It would not be long, however, before Blackman unsuspectingly embarked on a new career as commentator. 'I was at a North Glos motorcycle meeting one day and the commentator hadn't turned up. So they put a plea out over the PA system for someone to go and read the results. I'd never commentated before but I'd been in the music industry playing in bands, so I was used to a microphone. So that was where the commentating started,' he says. Indeed, it was a sidecar race that nearly ended Blackman's career behind the microphone. 'The one and only time I nearly swore on air was during a sidecar race. I was commentating at Old Paddock and a chap called Kenny Howells was leading on the first lap. He spun on the first lap in front of the entire pack and I nearly swore. I said to him afterwards that I had nearly sworn and he said: 'I did swear!'

At the conclusion of the 1981 season, three more circuit features were permanently named. The fast left-hander on the approach to Tower was appropriately named Hammerdown, the right-hand sweep after the start was called Folly and the kink on Dean Straight became West Way.

'The recommendation from the inspector was that if we behaved ourselves it should be reviewed in the light of experience in two years for a possible increase of another two days. We won an award of costs for vexatious action against the County Council which was quite unique at the time. Meanwhile the circuit was just carrying on, but there had been no development. We'd just been treading water, but it never failed to stagger me

Roger Orgee (March) sits on a Formula Libre grid in the early 1980s.

just how popular the place was. We'd achieved a likeable country cousin image,' reckons Strawford.

The 1981 season started on Easter Monday with a nine-race programme. The fact that the temporary interim planning had only been granted a week earlier meant that the BRSCC team went into the meeting with a sense of relief. Notable in the local special saloon car race was a one-two in the 1300cc class for father and son duo Brian and Tony Cutting. Veteran racer Brian also won the race overall while young Tony was just starting out in racing. In July, the biggest meeting of the season included Formula Ford 2000 and Sports 2000 championship rounds, won by Simon Kirkby (Reynard 81SF) and John Sheldon (Tiga SC81) respectively.

In August, a chapter of Castle Combe history closed with the death of caretaker Bill Little. Having worked minor miracles to tend the circuit over a 20-year period on a minuscule budget, Bill had been a cornerstone of keeping the site up together even when its future looked bleak. Sadly, he died shortly after the circuit's future was finally secured.

For many years, Little had lived in Westway Farm and that would now become home for the Strawford family. 'In 1980 I was made redundant and I was quite well paid off. For 16 months I was paid my full salary not to work against my former company. I was able to put a lot of time into preparation for our next inquiry and it also meant that, with my redundancy money, I was able to

85

Ayrton Senna da Silva (Van Diemen RF82) at Quarry in 1982.

Photo: John Gaisford.

buy Westway Farm. It was a bit run down and didn't have electricity and water either. We gutted it, had it rebuilt and eventually moved in. Not only did we move into the house, we moved into the community. I signed the family on with the local doctor which was quite significant as he was the vice-chairman of the local objectors' group,' says Strawford.

'My younger daughter Emma went to the local junior school and we set about proving that we were just a reasonable family trying to run a family business. I ran it from a portakabin in the garden with Pat doing the race entries. I used to do all the management, all the supervision and sometimes a bit of the plumbing. I think the low point was rodding cess pits!'

For 1982 the eight days were used for seven BRSCC car meetings and a North Glos MCC motorcycle meeting. At the traditional early July meeting, glorious sunshine resulted in a glut of new lap records. Most significant of all was a new standard for Formula Ford 2000 as a young Brazilian demolished the existing standard. Back then, Ayrton Senna was still known as Ayrton Senna da Silva but he was already rocking the establishment with his speed in a Van Diemen RF82. He saw off the challenge of British ace Calvin Fish and beat the previous record on every one of 15 laps once the race was underway. Fish raced hard to stay close to the Brazilian and even matched the new record 1m02.6s, but it was another victory for the man who would go on to become one of the sport's all-time greats.

Towards the end of 1982, the time came to apply for the additional two days of racing that had been suggested when permanent planning had been granted. 'Needless to say, we behaved ourselves for two years and applied for two extra days. Would you believe, it went to appeal. But we did eventually get the extra two days to take us to 10 days racing a year,' says Strawford.

The Lotus Elans of Pat Thomas and Rob Cox battle into Camp.

Photo: Chris Harvey.

Despite support for the increase to 10 days from officials from North Wilts. District Council the initial application was rejected on grounds of noise following lobbying from the small local pressure group. A council report even stated there was insufficient evidence to reject the proposal on grounds of noise emission. The public inquiry was finally held in December 1983. 'Tony Whatmore from Southampton University was called in as an expert witness. The case was won but the circuit also won a subsequent appeal for costs against North Wilts. District Council for vexatious action,' recalls Strawford. Meanwhile, the 1983 season had once more centred on seven BRSCC meetings and a motorcycle meeting.

Big event of the 1983 season was a meeting in September that included rounds of the RAC British Formula Ford 1600 and British Formula Ford 2000 Championships. Andrew Gilbert-Scott (Lola T642E) won the FF1600 contest while Welsh ace Tim Davies topped the 2-litre category in his Reynard 83SF.

The increasing circuit activity dictated an increase in office space and an additional member for the team. 'We

rebuilt some outbuildings at Westway Farm into an office block and ran it all from there. I was then going to advertise for someone to come and do the office work, but I ended up taking on our elder daughter Karen. She was very, very central to most of the things we ran,' says Strawford. 'By now Mrs Thomas was in her mid-70s and I had been trying to help sort out the estate. It had been in trust with solicitors running it for about 60 years. I tackled her about the possibility of buying the freehold as I was starting to wonder what would happen to it next. I managed to negotiate through the trustees to buy the circuit which was about 75 acres. We had been paying about £3000 a year rent but were able to buy it for around £57,000. That was the turning point of the whole operation. We bought the circuit, the run-off areas and the paddock.'

Finally in March 1984 came the news from the public inquiry that permanent planning permission had been granted for the two extra days' racing each year. From the start of the 1985 season, the circuit would be able to hold racing on 10 days, double the number when Strawford took over the circuit more than a decade earlier. It had

Alo Lawler on his way to breaking the outright circuit record.

Photo: John Gaisford.

taken an enormous effort and substantial cost, but the battle had been won and the future of the circuit had never looked better.

Once again, the main event of the season came in July 1984 with a visit from the Racing Displays British Formula Ford 2000 Championship. In control of the pack right from the start of qualifying was Brazilian Mauricio Gugelmin who would later go on to race in Formula 1 and Champ Cars in America. He saw off the challenge of fellow Brazilian Maurizio Sandro Sala and Andy Wallace who would later be a Le Mans winner. Also in the pack was future Lotus grand prix driver Julian Bailey and

Gary, son of Jack, Brabham. That warm July day was also notable for the very first 120mph lap when Tony Trimmer broke the outright circuit record that had stood for 14 years. In John Jordan's Formula 5000 Lola T330, Trimmer slicked more than a second from the mark set by Peter Gethin and Howden Ganley when the Formula 5000 cars raced at Castle Combe in period. His best race lap of 55.2s represented exactly 120mph, although he had lapped under the 55s mark in qualifying.

As 1985 opened, the news broke that the circuit had won costs against North Wilts. District Council. The award was made by the Secretary of State for the

Department of the Environment and represented a five-figure campaign by the circuit. 'I feel like the cat that's got the cream. This is a most worthwhile victory for motor sport as a whole and in the South West in particular,' said Strawford at the time. In 1985, the ten days would include seven BRSCC meetings, one 750MC meeting and two motorcycle meetings.

In April, Vince Woodman and Jonathan Buncombe teamed up in the former's Cologne Capri to win the two-part Thundersaloon race, while in May Canadian Bertrand Fabi won a round of the British Formula Ford 2000 Championship. Two months later Avon celebrated 100 years of tyre manufacture by supporting the July meeting and the outright circuit record was again broken. In qualifying for the Formula Libre race, Trimmer took the Lola T3330 around in 53.9s and went on to win the 20-lap race despite concerns over tyres. But he lost his year-old record to the pursuing Alo Lawler in his McLaren M30 Grand Prix car. The Lancastrian plant hire boss had raced Formula Ford extensively before acquiring the McLaren to race in Formula Libre events

and his speed that day set a new record in 54.2s (122.21mph) that would survive for more than 12 years.

In September a double-header for the British Formula Ford 1600 and Formula Ford 2000 Championships brought half a dozen future grand prix drivers to the circuit. In the FF2000 race, Fabi won again to beat Martin Donnelly as a rain shower brought the race to a premature halt. But it was the Formula Ford 1600 pack that was the most remarkable, with five drivers who would later become Formula 1 stars including Damon Hill. Brazilian Paulo Carcasci won the race narrowly from Belgian Bertrand Gachot while Hill was down in sixth place. Johnny Herbert just pipped Mark Blundell for eighth while Eddie Irvine was back in 14th! Blundell had been at the head of the action but an incident with Gachot cost Blundell a lot of time. After the race there was a heated exchange in the paddock but a policeman happened to be close at hand and came between them. Blundell was later fined and had his licence endorsed for causing the affray and then protested Gachot's driving. After long deliberations, the Belgian had his licence

Damon Hill and Jeremy Packer leave the grid, September 1985.

Photo: John Gaisford.

endorsed and was reprimanded over his driving standards.

Carcasci showed his mastery of the circuit in May 1986 when, having stepped up to Formula Ford 2000, he won again while Johnny Herbert retired the unloved Quest SF86. Despite racing with, and beating, many drivers who would later gain Formula 1 fame, Carcasci proved to be one of the lost talents of the generation.

While the 1986 season was in full swing, Strawford and his team were opening negotiations about the next phase of land acquisition. The particular land that Strawford wanted was that adjacent to Old Paddock and running down to Tower. At the time, the circuit owned none of the land immediately behind the safety banking and so spectator access was not possible. Indeed, the safety bank really needed to be moved further back as cars were occasionally finding their way over the bank and into the adjoining field.

'The area adjacent to Old Paddock corner and down to Tower was now owned by Mrs Thomas' daughter-in-law, who was now divorced from Mrs Thomas' son. She offered to sell me something like 200 acres at £2000 an acre. I indicated that there was no way I could raise £400,000. The next I heard was that the land was going to be offered for sale in lots. Lot 1 was the piece inside the circuit and there were various lots down around Old Paddock right down to Kents Bottom Farm, and the farm was part of it. That was how I came to know Maurice Avent, who owns the valley that runs on from the back of Tower corner,' remembers Strawford.

'A lot of farmers were interested in the land in the centre of the circuit and kept coming and asking what rights of way there were across the circuit. Of course, there weren't any so these potential buyers disappeared and it all went very quiet. About six months later the three parties interested in various parts of the 200 acres came to a deal and we got the land that we wanted for the circuit. We got the long narrow piece of land behind Old Paddock and Hammerdown that joined up with the car park area at Quarry, which enabled us to construct the viewing bank and the access road behind it. We trebled the run-off at Old Paddock before the 1988 season

because that had become the Achilles heel for the circuit in safety terms. We also obtained the lot known as Old Paddock at a sensible price because it was totally land-locked. It was covered in the remains of buildings with no access and had been derelict for 20 years, so we bought it and developed it over the years as a skid pan and kart circuit,' says Strawford. Additionally, some resurfacing was done and when the season opened spectators could, for the first time, walk all round the circuit.

'One way or another, we eventually brought the whole jigsaw back together. In about 1988 we bought the centre of the circuit and that totals about 137 acres of which we use about 25 acres for run-off areas, leaving over 110 acres of farmland. We rent that out to a local farmer and it is an arrangement that works extremely well,' says Strawford.

The progress being made at the circuit had been amply demonstrated in the summer of 1986 when press rumours linked Castle Combe with John Foulston's ambition to acquire a fourth circuit. Having already bought Brands Hatch, Oulton Park and Snetterton, Foulston was rumoured to be pursuing the Wiltshire track. But Strawford was quick to stress that the circuit was not for sale. Later, Strawford confirmed that he received a series of offers from the Foulston family, but, as had always been the case, the circuit was not for sale.

In 1987 the entry for a round of the Star of Tomorrow Formula Ford 1600 Championship in August included a pair of young Scots with a big future in the sport. Allan McNish finished fourth and would go on to become a world-renowned sportscar racer and 1998 Le Mans winner. One place behind him in that race was Paul Stewart, son of triple world champion Jackie. His own racing career would take him up to Formula 3000 before, along with his father, Paul set up the Stewart Grand Prix team. McNish also raced in the circuit's own Formula Ford race and beat off the local experts to take the chequered flag.

At the same meeting, the Pacific Racing team caused some problems when, after working late into Friday night changing engines on the cars of JJ Lehto and Jason

Beyond the point of no return for a Formula Ford driver at Quarry.

Photo: Steve Jones.

Elliott, they started the engines in the paddock in the small hours of the morning. For a circuit with local opposition it was a serious matter and team boss Keith Wiggins was called to account in the morning. He offered a formal apology and the stewards decided to take no further action. But the circuit made a plea for teams to respect local villagers at all times.

In November 1987 another chapter in the Castle Combe circuit history came to an end when Mrs Thomas died at the age of 82. She had been a formidable lady who had consistently championed the cause of the circuit. There is no question that her determination and spirit to keep the circuit alive had been vital in it surviving the first 30 years. Once she realised it was in safe hands with Howard Strawford, Mrs Thomas was finally able to step back from the day to day running of the venue.

Around this time, Strawford also recognised that the whole venture was growing in volume of activity and decided that some expert opinion on the business would

be sensible. 'The Department of Trade and Industry was running a campaign to 'put a bit of whoosh' into your company. We'd reached a stage where the circuit was doing quite well. The racing school had developed into running novice days and we used to hire the cars in from Graham Taylor and Mike Knight used to oversee it. But we had planning to run quite a few racing school days and we were only running about half a dozen a year. So I started renting out the circuit to other people to run racing schools. I knew in my heart of hearts that it was the wrong thing to do because, apart from anything else, we used to regularly get complaints from disgruntled customers,' recalls Strawford.

'So we had a consultant from the DTI and he did a superb study for us. He suggested that we revamp the racing school and make a lot more of it and didn't allow anyone else to operate a racing school from the venue because it was just giving us a bad name. The number one proposition he came out with was that we should build in the centre of the circuit a massive museum dedicated to the history of motor racing. He told me that

91

because it was a cash rich company we could borrow up to £5 million to build this museum! I would never be sold on that idea.

'Having said that, his proposals two to nine were very, very good. A little bit hurtful, mind you. Proposals two, three and four were based upon the fact that we couldn't expect to extend the operation of our business with the state of our toilet facilities. He was unmerciful on this one. Proposals five, six and seven were about the racing school and were very good. We have since adopted those in the biggest possible way and we now run 40 days a year with 100 people each day.

'We had revamped the existing toilets quite extensively. When we took over the circuit, the toilets at the circuit were of the type that made you go at home before you set out. Unfortunately, during that first meeting I had to use the gents in race control. I was ensconced in the cubicle and I was more than somewhat surprised to find that someone else was desperate to use the same cubicle. He pushed hard on the door handle and, to my amazement, broke the top hinge on the door which fell down and hit me on the head. I looked over this door, he said 'sorry mate' and disappeared, leaving me trying to close the door and regain some dignity. I regarded that as a sign that we should do something about the toilets. The toilets that were installed in the 1950s were built mainly

Toyota Formula 3 action at Tower in 1988.

Photo: John Gaisford.

Formula Libre racing in 1989 with Eddie McLurg's Minardi to the fore.

Photo: Doug Rees.

from about 3000 doors from the blitz clearance in Bristol. They put together four by two frames and clad the outside in doors. They did paint them all the same colour, I will admit.

'Anyway, I hired in an architect to have a look at the toilets and he came up with a pretty good idea which was to use the black and white tiles. That was one of the first major investments we made and it was about £60,000 just for the paddock. We went on to convert all the rest to portakabins but it took a couple of years as we had to lay miles of water pipe,' says Strawford.

The 1988 season opened with the extended run-off area at Old Paddock giving drivers more room for error and in May the British Formula Ford 1600 Championship round was won by rising British star Derek Higgins. In fourth place was Mexican Adrian

Fernandez, who would later make his name in Champ Car racing. But the 1988 season was also marked by two of the more bizarre events in Castle Combe's racing history. In July, Porsche racer Rod Webster was black-flagged for driving too slowly! Having previously crashed the car heavily at Brands, Webster was called before the stewards after qualifying when it became apparent that he was lapping more than 12 seconds slower than anyone else in the field. His steady pace continued in the race and he was shown the black flag several times, but failed to stop. Later, he claimed that lack of race experience and poor visibility caused him to miss the flag, but the officials were not impressed and he was excluded from the results, fined £100 and had his licence endorsed for ignoring the flag.

Then, in September, Super Road Saloon racer Jeff Stimson staged what is thought to be the only race

The return of national motor cycle racing. Carl Fogarty heads the pack at Quarry.
Photo: Paul Korkus.

Young Scot David Coulthard waves to the crowd after victory on May 29th, 1989.
Photo: John Gaisford.

control sit-in protest in the circuit's history. A mix up over entries by a race entry service he was using left him only a reserve for the race. Clerk of the Course Bob Llewellyn tried to solve the problem and eventually Richard Waller gave up his place on the grid so that Stimpson could compete.

Having existed for 38 years without a permanent pit road, work began early in 1989 to construct a pit entry road starting at the entrance to Camp Corner and running past the Avon Bridge to a wide working area just past race control. Soon into the construction work came the first accident of the season when two dumper trucks collided. Fortunately damage was light and no one was injured, so work continued as planned. This important new facility was inaugurated in August 1989 when it was used in anger during a round of the Thundersaloon Championship. The race was won by the familiar pairing of Woodman and Buncombe, this time in the 6-litre Vauxhall Carlton.

Earlier in the season, a young Scottish racer had set the Star of Tomorrow Formula Ford 1600 Championship alight by winning superbly on his graduation from karts. When the championship arrived at Castle Combe in May, David Coulthard continued his winning form. In July, Brazilian Gil de Ferran won the British Formula Ford 1600 Championship race and he and Coulthard would go on to become great friends as they climbed the racing ladder together. While Coulthard graduated to Formula 1, De Ferran carved a successful career racing Champ Cars in America.

The 1989 season also marked the return of national motorcycle racing for the first time in nearly 20 years as the New Era Motor Cycle Club hosted the April meeting. Young Carl Fogarty blasted the lap record on his way to winning the 750 race on his Honda. His new record of 102.22mph represented the first recorded 100mph motor cycle lap of the circuit. At the same meeting, Mick Boddice and Chas Birks set the first 100mph sidecar lap on their Yamaha and lopped a whole eight seconds off the previous mark that Boddice had held jointly with Chris Vincent.

Chapter 8

The 1990s

-

development and growth

The new decade began with a sharp and unexpected wake-up call from the North Wilts. District Council when, immediately into the New Year, mid-week testing for racing cars was cut from 20 days a year to just four following the threat of serving a Noise Nuisance Order. A negotiated settlement was reached in May based on a compromise of eight days' race testing each year instead of four.

In March 1990, planning permission was granted for a new timekeepers' and commentary tower to be built on top of the race control building. The previous structure had been a casualty of the gales that devastated the country at the end of the previous year. 'We made major improvements to the race control building over the years, including constructing the timekeepers' building. That was the top floor originally, but it was blown away in the gales. The council agreed to give us planning permission to replace it, which we did. That gave us a ruling from the council as to what they considered a decent building as far as roofing material was concerned,' says Strawford. Then, in October, temporary planning permission was granted for one sprint for road-silenced vehicles.

Modified Saloon action into Tower with Derek Hales at the forefront.

Photo: Steve Jones.

'We still attracted the interest of the environmental health people who were doing numerous noise tests. I was quite devastated here one day to be served an environmental protection order, which we decided to appeal largely because we were doing most of the required work. We were building the noise bunds and the first thing that the order said was that we had to build the noise bunds. We were already doing it.

'We went to appeal and used the same barrister. We half won it and got it significantly modified. We went on to build the noise bunds but had to obtain retrospective planning permission for it! The planning came with landscaping conditions and a condition saying we couldn't have any advertising or fencing on them. The Sainsbury's bank between Quarry and Old Paddock, so named as it was built from the soil cleared from the site of a new supermarket in Chippenham, was five metres high. If you fell down that you could break your neck so we fenced it in a very expensive way with rustic fencing. But I'll never regret that because it looks so good. The banks at Tower and Camp were built from soil cleared from the site of a Safeways supermarket,' recalls Strawford.

'We got into terrible difficulty with the landscaping. We got a landscaping firm in but they didn't take account of the quality of the subsoil and the whole lot died. It didn't take long before we were reminded by the planners that if the plants die, you've got to replace them. And they died again. So we replaced them again. And they died again. We were supposed to replace them with the same species. This was three years down the road and the bank was looking as bald as a coot. So I just decided we'd plant what we wanted to plant on it. I planted Cypressus and I got into a bit of trouble about that. The landscaping was a very, very big job and we have spent many tens of thousands of pounds on it.

'The re-vamp of the whole operation meant that we had to take on more and more staff and we were out-growing the space at Westway House. So we had to get proper offices. But the local authority wanted us to build an award winning office. We couldn't get planning permission for what I would call a utilitarian office block. It had to be an elaborate building,' says Strawford.

Bob Giles, who would be central to the resurfacing project in 1992, was also a well qualified management consultant. 'We were now employing six people full time and the business was growing a lot faster than I was happy with, so I asked Bob if he would like to do a management study on us. The first thing he said was that we had to build new offices. Martin Chick had encouraged me to get the planning for the fancy new offices with a view to me appealing them to bring down the cost. But Bob Giles said go for it, and that's what we did. It was the most extraordinarily expensive office to build, but we did it. He organised us quite significantly from a management point of view,' says Strawford.

'It was also apparent that I needed to employ somebody on the marketing side and it was co-incidental that Rodney Gooch who I'd known for some time as a good friend, was available. He came part-time initially but over a five year period I managed to persuade him to come full time as marketing and promotion manager.' For Gooch, it was a return to a circuit he had raced on during his motorcycle career. 'I stopped racing in 1971 and went off to Australia to seek fame and fortune. I came back with neither fame nor fortune but had a wonderful time,' says Gooch.

On his return to Britain he started working as sales manager for Aerosigns, at the time the company with contracts for erecting trackside signs at many British circuits. 'I remember crashing into one of their signs at Brands and smashing the bike up more than me.' That gave me an involvement back at Castle Combe because Aerosigns had a contract with Howard. I stayed at Aerosigns until immediately after the last British Grand Prix there in 1986, when John Webb offered me a job to go and work at Brands where I stayed until 1991.

'I set up on my own then and I'd known Howard for many years. Although he didn't have a full time job, there were certain things he wanted doing and it suited both of us for me to work at the circuit on a part-time basis. He probably felt at the time that some more colour around the circuit would bring it alive more, because this is a colourful sport. First of all, I was working to get some signage around the place and then as the recession eased, the corporate market came back stronger,' recalls Gooch.

Steve Spray, Trevor Nation and John Reynolds, the first three in the Formula 1 race, 1990.

Photo:
Paul Korkus.

John Reynolds in the Supersports 600 race, April 1990.

Photo:
Paul Korkus.

Formula 1 action at Quarry, April 1990.

Photo:
Paul Korkus.

The April 1990 national motor cycle meeting brought another new outright circuit record as Steve Spray lapped his JPS Norton in 1m03.2s, an average speed of 104.81mph. Spray won the Formula One race from team mate Trevor Nation with John Reynolds third on a works Kawasaki. One of the most significant races for cars of the 1990 season was the September round of the British Formula Ford 1600 Championship, won by the under-rated Dutchman Michael Vergers in a Van Diemen RF90.

For 1991 the programme again centred on BRSCC meetings, of which there were nine, and a single motor cycle meeting again run by the New Era club. James Whitham (Suzuki) and Ray Stringer (Yamaha) trimmed a tenth of a second from Spray's year old circuit record. Like Carl Fogarty a couple of years earlier, Whitham would race at the circuit before his career took him to the very top of the sport. On four wheels there was tragedy in August 1991 when Special GT racer Alan Woodridge had the clutch explode on his Ford-powered Metro. He was very badly injured by the shrapnel and died 17 days later.

As the 1991 season concluded, major plans were being laid for a complete resurfacing of the circuit, even though the cost of such work would be a vast undertaking for the company. New for the 1992 season was the creation of the Castle Combe Racing School Ltd, which was owned by the circuit and managed by racer Alan Cooper. Along with Howard and Pat Strawford and daughter Karen, Cooper and Rodney Gooch became directors of the company. It was the beginning of a highly successful venture and replaced the previous school activities that had been run by various organisations over a 30-year period. 'We contracted with Alan to provide the product and concentrated on the marketing,' says Strawford.

Having been active at the circuit virtually since it opened for motorsport, Terry Sanger continued to be a senior instructor. Dealing with the general public can be unpredictable, but one occasion left a lasting impression on Sanger and fellow instructors Hugh Elliott and Roly Hamblin.

'We had a guy turn up at the school with a VW Polo,' recalls Sanger. 'He'd got bird song recorded onto a cassette tape and played the bird song to the car. He reckoned that this bird song aligned all the molecules in the car, the tyres, the brakes, the engine, the suspension and so on. He said that the car would run faster, corner faster, brake better and use less fuel as long as you had done this operation with the bird song tape. I was doing some test driving for Rover at the time and he wanted me to get Rover to play this tape to the cars while they were parked in storage.

'He wanted to test the car on the circuit. So we let him out onto the track and told him to take it steady. He came down to Camp, hit a puddle and went straight into the bank. He bent the wing and broke the mirrors and scraped the paint off. He got out and said: Those damn monks, they're praying against me again!' he then picked all the rubbish up, put it in the car and limped off with a bent wheel. We never saw him again.'

As well as the racing school, the kart circuit adjacent to Old Paddock was now established under the guidance of Steven Roberts, the founder of the Merlin Motorsport. Having enjoyed great success as a racer in Modsports championships, Roberts later developed the Sports 2000-based Merlin Exocet for the Castle Combe Special GT Championship before stopping racing in 1986 when business got too busy. Roberts previously worked for Midas Cars and then Marcos where he started an operation called Speedex. From there, he created Merlin Motorsport at the Castle Combe circuit to supply competition and performance accessories. 'It was difficult to race at Castle Combe without people coming and asking questions all the time. In the end, I wasn't doing either justice so it was better to stop racing,' he recalls.

His company has since expanded to add the skid pan and karting operations as well as the 4x4 off-road course. The operation now has 10 full-time staff and another 20 part-timers, mainly instructors. 'We have an MSA-registered kart track and we do a lot with juniors,' says Roberts. Some of the early graduates of the kart school are now starting to move into Formula Ford at the circuit.

A packed grid of MG Midgets sets off in the early 1990s.

'It is useful for Merlin to be based on the circuit. I don't think any other circuit has an accessory shop on site these days. We are open six days a week and on all race days. At race meetings, we tend to be only busy during the mornings. We do a lot of chaos-sorting when the scrutineers find a problem on a car. We then go rushing around trying to sort out the panic, or people have had an off in qualifying and need rose joints and tank tape,' says Roberts.

Back in June 1992, John Reynolds smashed the outright motor cycle record on his 750 Kawasaki and took the new mark down to 1m01.8s, an average speed of 107.18mph. This was the fourth improvement in four years and represented an increase in average speeds of nearly 20mph in 30 years. However, in November work was started that was likely to increase speeds still further as Strawford and Bob Davies set about organising and funding a complete resurfacing programme.

'Bob Davies and I worked closely together and I was greatly worried about the cost of resurfacing. The first quotation I had was over £400,000 and we didn't have any cash behind us. I wanted to know how we were going to fund it, because it obviously had to be done. At that time, Bob came up with a very useful idea. If we took out

a fairly substantial pension fund, we could borrow the money from the fund to resurface when the time came,' says Strawford.

'There is a lot more to resurfacing than meets the eye. One thing I had learned was how to make the old surface last by patching it up. We'd had a few patches done quite successfully by a company called Wootton Tarpaving. But we'd also had a second lane surfaced by the scrutineering bay by a less reputable company and it was an absolute disaster. So, not being shy, I rang the head highways man at the County Council and he said: 'I'll be over in 20 minutes!' He soon got that sorted out and the work was re-done properly. In that line of business, if you are blacklisted by him, you're finished. So I took his advice about contractors for resurfacing the circuit and he explained that, as a result of local authority re-organisation, they had started a direct services department and could handle the work themselves. I liked the sound of that. However, within 48 hours I had a letter from the council solicitor saying they did not want to get involved with the circuit, bearing in mind the position on the planning front.

'I then had a call from the highways man who recommended three or four other companies as well as a

Alex Rogan's Capri amidst Road Saloon confusion at Quarry.

Photo: Steve Jones.

Local Caterham racer Guy Parry heads the field in 1993.

consultant called Bob Giles. We went out to tender and the tenders were delivered here on the designated day. Being a cynical bastard, I opened these tenders and said to myself, these people have had lunch! The prices were surprisingly close and surprisingly high. One was particularly high and I couldn't understand that. I thought perhaps only three of them had been at the lunch. When I spoke to Bob Giles, it transpired that the company that was surprisingly high was owned by one of the others and was so busy that it didn't need the work. It had just put in a high price to make the others seem competitive. So I told them all to sod off! But I had a liking for Geoff Shearn from a firm called Ford Brothers and we eventually agreed a better price,' recalls Strawford.

The work was carried out in November 1992 when the old surface was completely re-engineered. The pit lane was widened and improved to double its old size. It was the first time that the circuit had been fully resurfaced since 1962 and other work included the concrete sections on the exit of Old Paddock being replaced by rumble strips.

'I also used Bob Giles to oversee the construction of the spectator banks at Tower and Camp. These were to prove lucrative for the circuit, for finding locations to dump the spoil from new construction sites is no easy task. The circuit gained financially and also got new spectator banks. We earned £30,000 from those two banks alone. Of course, we had to landscape and fence them, but it was a good earner. The only problem that we had was slippage in both of them and this was because the angles were too steep. In order to cure a problem of slippage, you can do one of two things. You either put weight on or take weight off. We opted to take some away and re-engineer, with a flat shelf part way down. At Tower, we had to get the bank back from next door and that was a massive engineering feat,' recalls Strawford, after slippage had sent some of the bank sliding through the boundary fence.

The new surface was christened in the spring of 1993 as the new season got underway but the team was not about to rest on its laurels. Over the winter of 1993/94, a major extension was added to the medical centre. A generous donation from the family of the late Ian McArdell helped the project considerably. Tragically, Ian

had died in October 1991 during the final round of the circuit's Formula Ford 1600 Championship. He was battling for the title with local veteran Bob Higgins when he crashed on Farm Straight and suffered fatal head injuries.

At the same time, the paddock area was extended to a total of nine acres by incorporating a section of the Chippenham Road car park into the paddock, just to the left of the main paddock entrance. The ever-growing number of entries together with the increasing trend, even in club racing, for teams to have trucks with awnings as their bases meant that the paddock was regularly bursting at the seams on race days. In April 1994 the new administration centre was completed and formally opened, but Strawford now had his sights set on attracting a round of the British Touring Car Championship to Wiltshire. With huge manufacturer support and massive crowds, the BTCC was riding on a crest of popularity and Strawford was keen to bring the series to Castle Combe. But a pre-requisite of that would be planning permission to run a two-day race meeting. As had become traditional for the circuit's applications, it went to appeal and was eventually successful with another award of costs in favour of the circuit.

'We must have been gluttons for punishment. After all the difficulties on the planning front we must have been mad to go ahead with an application to run two-day race meetings. At the same time we applied for permission for two more of what we call the public dealer days which are used to run the very popular action days. Would you believe they turned them down and they both went to appeal. Our previous barrister had retired, but we were still working with Martin Chick.

'Martin explained that there were about 30 barristers who now specialised in planning law, the top ten of which were all earning over £500,000 a year. That frightened me to death! But Martin was quite keen to hire one from the next 20. So I said I'd go along with that, as long as we were well away from the half a million brigade. We finished the discussion and Martin went home, but within about an hour he rang me back. He said he didn't ask me the key question. Did I want a rottweiler or a gentleman? I said: 'Don't be a pratt, we live in the village,' recalls Strawford.

Rod Birley (Honda Prelude) heads the Vauxhall Carlton of Pete Stevens in a 1993 Thundersaloon race.

'Geoffrey Stephenson was the man we chose and he was so impressed by everything we were doing to try and live with the neighbours, that he christened us Europe's most neighbour-friendly circuit. Perhaps amusingly, that was not challenged by the opposition. So that tag has stuck. We went on and won that appeal. The aim, as everyone knows, was to attract the British Touring Car Championship which we didn't succeed in doing. That was what we wanted when we went for two-day meetings. We couldn't ask for a BTCC round until we could run two-day meetings. But the weekend meetings have gone on to be immensely successful without touring cars.

'As a result of good housekeeping and the management of noise, we reached the stage where usage is now up to 250 days a year having started with five. It's more than enough to satisfy us. More to the point, that was only five race days originally and we've now got that up to 12, which is all I ever asked the planners to do in the first place. My aim was to get the usage up to the level of Thruxton and in fact we have exceeded that. In planning, you can only really decide on anything by balancing the harms against the benefits. The circuit now generates in excess of £15 million in the local economy,

which is a lot more than six NIMBYs with typewriters. In 1995 we even set up a local liaison committee, with members of the local parish councils involved. The circuit lies in both Castle Combe and Yatton Keynell parishes,' says Strawford.

The first two-day meeting was held in September 1995 and was a great success. Subsequently, two-day meetings have been held in July and September each year and have witnessed some of the best racing in the circuit's history. Often topped by races for the mighty TVR Tuscans, the two-day meetings have featured vast entries, more than 400 cars on at least one occasion.

In 1996, Rodney Gooch finally took a full-time position within the circuit management team. 'Gradually the role changed and I moved to Castle Combe full-time in 1996. It had got to the stage where the circuit needed someone full-time, so it was a case of the right place at the right time. It's a wide-ranging brief and that makes it so interesting. Every phone call can be different. It's great to be part of a huge success story and nice to be part of the team. We're really motorsport enthusiasts first and businessmen second.

Typically close Caterham action at Quarry.

The Ferrari pack sets off in the summer of 1997.

Always a crowd pleaser! The Caterham Roadsports descend on Old Paddock.
Photo: Steve Jones.

Formula Fords dive into Camp, 1997.

Kevin Mills and Richard Carter head a typical Formula Ford pack into Old Paddock.
Photo: Steve Jones.

The new circuit layout, introduced for the 1999 season.

Photo: Steve Jones.

Bobbies was introduced on West Way.

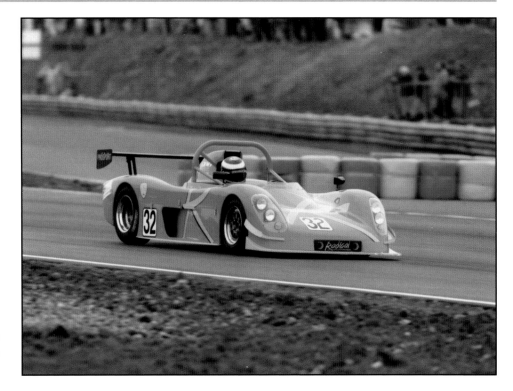

Michael Vergers (Radical Prosport) starred in the Special GT race in March 1999.

Photo: Steve Clarke.

Mini Miglia winners (from left to right) Steve Bell, Peter Baldwin and Ian Curley are joined by Sharon Bricknell on the winners' vehicle in July 1999.

Bob Light (B6 Sport) was the fastest man on the revised circuit in 1999.

Photo: Steve Clarke.

Champion elect Warren Hughes leads the MGF pack in August 1999.

Photo: Steve Clarke.

Ferraris dice into Quarry in 1999.

Photo: John Gaisford.

Mini Se7en racer Alan Letts searches for the problem, July 1999.

Photo: Steve Clarke.

John Moon (Calibra) and Grant Woodhatch (VW Vento) lead the Pagid Saloon pack out of the Esses in 1999. Photo: John Gaisford.

Mike Jordan heads Martin Short in a TVR Tuscan battle, July 1999.

Photo: Steve Clarke.

Porsche racers David Jones, Peter Chambers, Godfrey Jones, Chris Heeley and Richard True race through Tower, July 1999.

Photo: Steve Clarke.

The Mini Se7en pack disagrees on lines into the Esses, July 1999.

Photo: Steve Clarke.

Eurocar V8s in September 1999. Mark Willis heads Barry Lee, Kevin Clarke and Chris Dawkins.

Photo: Steve Clarke.

Ian McKellar Jnr
leads Phil
Hindley and
Michael Caine in
a TVR Tuscan
battle,
September 1999.

Photo:
Steve Clarke.

Pickup Trucks
racing on the
Eurocar package
in 1999.

Photo:
Steve Clarke.

Richard Carter leads the Formula Fords over Avon Rise, October 1999.
Photo: James Beckett.

Mick Hyde's Radical turns into Tower, October 1999.
Photo: James Beckett.

Chris Sanders (Lotus Cortina) heads Graeme Dodd (Jaguar Mk11), Roger Cope (Jaguar S Type) and Jim Utting (Ford Mustang) into Quarry, October 1999.

Photo: Steve Jones.

The final meeting of 1999 marked the very first T-Car races. Tom Boardman (pictured) won all three races.

Photo: Steve Clarke.

November 1999. The circuit makes a donation towards the new play area at Yatton Keynell.

June 1999, the marriage of Emma Strawford and Steve Burns. From left to right: Howard Strawford, Pat Strawford, Steve Burns, Emma Burns, Graham Marshallsay, Karen Marshallsay with George Marshallsay at the front. Photo: Alan Cassé

Rick Hall demonstrates the BRM V16 during the August 1994 classic meeting.

Andy Blackman (with microphone) and Steve Parrish (centre) on the startline in 1994.

A mammoth Mini Seven grid prepares for battle in 1994.

Ian Allwood makes a hasty exit from his hot Morgan at Tower in 1994.

September 1995. A typical TVR Tuscan grid heads for Folly.

Photo: John Gaisford.

Tuscan aces Ian Flux and Martin Short battle through Camp.

Photo: John Gaisford.

Caterham Roadsports thrill the crowd in 1996.

Nigel Greensall powers through Quarry on his way to the lap record.

Photo: Steve Jones.

'When I came to Castle Combe from Brands, I couldn't quite believe the crowds. I thought Brands would do it bigger and better than anyone, but when I came down here I wondered where all these people had come from. August Bank Holiday Monday was the first meeting I came to and I was staggered with the numbers. Also, I couldn't get over how quickly the club ran the meeting. We do give value for money to our sponsors and to our spectators,' says Gooch.

'By 1996 we had finished paying off all the loans on the land we had bought and the circuit totalled 220 acres,' says Strawford. 'So we started a fairly big refurbishment, most notably of the toilets. We rebuilt five toilet blocks in two years. We've used the same architect for the buildings and he took us into a definitive style, so we don't have buildings that are unsympathetic to the others and the countryside. They have all been built with comparatively indigenous materials.

'In recent seasons we have refurbished all the paddock buildings and re-roofed them. It has been a constant programme of investment. The re-roofing programme alone ran to more than a quarter of a million pounds. And the toilet blocks cost a similar amount. We also rebuilt the old ambulance shed and created the clock tower. The clock is the one that was on race control at Brands Hatch and we bought it from the scrap dealer, so it's got a bit of history. We bought it for a pound, but it cost us thousands to get it going again.'

On the racing front, the annual motor cycle meeting was dogged by bad weather even though it had taken a firm hold on a June date. But it was dry enough in 1996 for Graham Ward (Ducati) to set a new lap record at 107.86mph, four tenths of a second beneath John Reynolds' four-year-old standard.

At the close of the 1996 season, a period of Castle Combe history came to a close when circuit commentator Richard Davies hung up his microphone and moved to Spain. Having been the voice of Castle Combe for 20 years, it marked the end of an era when he commentated for the final time at the last meeting of 1996. Indeed, he was sorely missed by many regular fans and the circuit even launched a publicity campaign to find a replacement for the popular character.

In August 1997, the outright circuit record was re-written in the most spectacular style. The BOSS series, open to a wide range of powerful single-seater racing cars, was headed by Nigel Greensall in a former grand prix Tyrrell 022 entered by Paul Stoddart's European Aviation Racing team. Greensall, a regular racer and winner at Castle Combe in a wide range of cars, rose to the challenge and smashed the circuit record by lapping in 50.59s, an average of 130.93mph. It was a stunning display that thrilled the bumper Bank Holiday crowd and would make Greensall the all-time fastest driver in the circuit's history. The circuit changes instigated before the 1999 season ensured that his record would not be broken.

'The first time I went to Castle Combe was in a Multisport in 1991,' says Greensall. 'Then I did Formula Forward and Formula Ford after that, but it was basically one race a year. Then I ran the ProSport 3000 there in 1995 and 1996. In August 1997, I was due to race the ProSport on the same day as the Formula 1 car, but the engine failed in qualifying.

'The number of people who turned up that day was fantastic. It was a shame in some ways, because we had a 20-minute untimed session and it was pouring with rain. Then the qualifying session was held in the wet, and although it wasn't raining so hard by then, the track was still soaking wet. So the first dry lap in the Tyrrell was the first lap of the race. Had it been dry in the morning there were a few things we would have done differently on the car, which would have found us more speed,' says Greensall.

'The main challenge in the race was Johan Rajamaki in the Arrows, but his engine failed before the race so there wasn't a serious threat in terms of speed. The big challenge then was to see how quick a lap we could do. The car ran well for the first two thirds of the race but then the gearbox started to fail and I was stuck in fifth gear. That cost us the chance of putting in an even quicker lap. It's frustrating to look back on it because we could have gone under the 50-second mark, but the lap time was still pretty good.

'It was a fantastic sensation racing that car at Castle Combe. In a car like that you obviously notice all the undulations in the surface and there were quite a few

The biggest ever ProSport 3000 field pours into Old Paddock.

Photo: Steve Jones.

occasions when the car was airborne. Looking at the data, there were quite a few spikes on the speed graphs. Up over Avon Rise we were getting airborne as the wheel speed graphs were showing 186mph but we were only actually doing 182mph, so the rear wheels were obviously skipping off the ground. It was sixth gear all the way from the startline to Avon Rise,' he says.

'Quarry was third gear before going back up to sixth and holding sixth through Old Paddock. I was braking very lightly for Old Paddock because in the race, I was able to be quite conservative as there wasn't a direct challenger. We were also trying to make sure of a finish as we were chasing the championship. I knew I'd got to get the car to the finish, as well as enjoy it and entertain people.

'The arrival speed at Old Paddock was 178mph and about 145mph turning through the corner. We then got

back up to just over 170mph down into Tower, which was a third gear corner. The peak speed on Dean Straight was 179mph before Camp. I tried Camp in fourth gear and fifth gear and it seemed to work better in fourth, although with a bit of work I think we could have got through Camp in fifth and got a better lap time. It just felt fantastic,' says Greensall.

'Castle Combe has always been how I feel racing should be. On reflection, it has made me realise I wish I'd been racing in the 1960s and early 1970s. I got such a buzz from it and it reminded me why I first got into motor racing. In some ways, I wish I'd been a spectator that day, because it would have been great to stand on the bank and be that close to a Formula 1 car travelling at those speeds. The crowd seemed to enjoy it. I'm a bit sad that the circuit has changed, because as a driver I loved the old lay-out. The danger is that as circuits get safer, driving standards drop, so it is nice to have the circuits like Castle Combe that are a real challenge. It was a real highlight for me and I'd love to go back there with a Formula 1 car.'

That same month, following the dropping of Kent-engined Formula Fords from the annual Formula Ford Festival at Brands Hatch, the BRSCC hosted the first Formula Ford Carnival at the circuit. Catering only for

Peter Cook's Ferrari F40 en route to disaster at Camp in July 1998.

Photo: John Gaisford.

In October 1997, the circuit made perhaps its boldest planning application to date. Now that Castle Combe Circuit Ltd owned all of the infield area, it seemed a logical step to pursue using some of those acres to improve facilities for circuit visitors. The only way to use it however, was to cross the circuit and so application was made to construct a bridge over the circuit to enable the infield to be used for car parking and for the creation of a hospitality area. The plan was that this area would be served by a new access road from the B4039 and would also require the construction of a 320 metre embankment. But this was rejected by the North Wilts District Council. 'One problem we have is that there is not enough parking at the circuit. We lost some spectator parking when the paddock was extended into the Chippenham Road car park. In the last couple of years we have come very close to being full for car parking at the Bank Holiday meetings,' said Strawford at the time.

the older Kent-engined cars, the Carnival was run over two heats and a final and, though it failed to attract substantial numbers, it was hotly contested by the regular local competitors and was won by Cornishman Richard Carter (Van Diemen RF92).

The 1998 season was one of enormous contrast. Crowds and race entries were bigger than ever as the circuit's popularity continued to boom. However, several major accidents put circuit safety under the spotlight and ultimately led to the introduction of circuit changes that Strawford had been planning before the season started.

In July, the Porsches of Godfrey Jones and Peter Chambers crashed dramatically at Camp after they had touched at the entry to the corner. While Chambers' Carrera 993 hit the bank backwards at high speed, the similar car of Jones went in head first at virtually

A vast Super Coupe pack descends on Quarry in 1998.

Photo: Steve Jones.

unabated speed. The Porsche burst through the top of the banking. It was a massive impact and witnesses were relieved that both drivers emerged unscathed, testimony in particular to the strength of the cars constructed by Mike Jordan's Team Eurotech.

Hot on the heels of that potentially serious accident came a freak tragedy. On August Bank Holiday Monday, the thundering TVR Tuscans were the star attraction. In qualifying, championship contender Bobby Verdon-Roe suffered a suspension failure on the approach to Camp and his car shed a wheel. While the car spun into the barriers without harm to the driver, the wheel bounced high over the banking and crashed down upon a spectator on the banking above the corner. Poor Lee Noble from Southampton suffered major injuries and could not be saved despite the immediate attention of the medical team. It was a genuinely freak accident that could have

happened at any venue in Britain, but the backlash added further weight to the prospect of circuit changes before the 1999 season.

In truth, Strawford had been working on plans to reduce speeds for some time, and certainly well before the high-profile accidents of that summer and plans had been drawn as early as 1997. 'It was clear that some championships were choosing not to come to Castle Combe simply because they felt it was too fast for them. Rather than be presented with a situation where we might make a knee-jerk reaction, we have been planning ahead for some time to find a satisfactory solution,' said Strawford when announcing the planned changes in September. Along with two new corners, the work also required the relocation of two marshals' posts and the provision of grass and paved run-off areas. The total cost ran to around £200,000.

Never miss a photo opportunity! Howard Strawford starts work on the new corners late in 1998.

December 1998 - Greensall and Strawford unveil the new corners.

Photo: Paul Lawrence.

Unveiled in December 1998, the circuit revisions featured two new corners designed to reduce speeds at critical points on the circuit. Just before Old Paddock was the Esses while between Tower and West Way was Bobbies, named in memory of Bob Davies who had been a central part of the management team right up until his untimely death in the summer of 1998.

The new corners, which added just under a tenth of a mile to the circuit length, had been designed by Stuart Michael Associates, a Newbury-based company that had already worked on extensive circuit changes at Silverstone. Bob Giles was civil engineering consultant on the project and the contractors were Ford Brothers of Cheddar. The new sections of track were surfaced in Trackphalte and the work involved approximately 2000 lorry loads of materials, including foundations. Remarkably, the work was completed 18 days ahead of schedule and was unveiled to the press on December 14.

Strawford's brief to the designers was to create proper corners rather than a swerve around little more than a tyre barrier. The planning process took account of the opinions of a large number of officials, drivers and riders as well as the sport's governing body, the Motor Sports Association. Initial computer predictions suggested that the entry speed to Old Paddock would be reduced by around 45mph and the entry to Camp Corner by around 20mph. An increase in lap times of around five seconds was expected.

During the unveiling process, when Strawford and Nigel Greensall cut the ribbon in front of the press, Strawford commented on the changes. 'Pressure has built up to make changes and the decision was taken in July. We could have built a horrible chicane on Farm Straight for £10,000, but we wanted to do it properly.' Greensall, after a first look at the corners, agreed that a fine job had been done. 'This has probably added to the challenge and it will be good for spectators. It's a lot of fun driving the new corners,' he said.

Radicals race through Bobbies, October 1999.

Photo: James Beckett.

Saloons head up towards the Esses in 1999.

Photo: James Beckett.

The new track layout was the most obvious change to the circuit for the 1999 season, but other work had also been completed. More tarmac roads and walkways would improve the facilities for spectators still further and the drivers' changing room in the paddock was also upgraded. The fans responded by packing the circuit for the early meetings in 1999 and it soon became apparent that the Esses was becoming a favourite viewing spot. In rapid response to this, the circuit team drew up plans to extend the spectator banking and quickly introduced a second level of viewing to enable up to another 500 fans to have a good view of the new corner. This work was completed in double quick time and was ready in time for the Spring Bank Holiday meeting at the end of May.

On four wheels, the first record for the revised 1.85-mile track was set during the inaugural meeting on Saturday March 20 1999. Contesting the Open Sportscar race, Mike Millard lapped his LM3000 in 1m05.61s, an average of 101.50mph. Through the spring and summer, however, it was local GT championship contender Bob Light who consistently set new records in his superb self-conceived Chevrolet-engined B6 Sport. From 1m05.13s on Easter Monday, by late August Light had progressively trimmed that to 1m03.389s, an average of 105.07mph. During the annual motor cycle meeting in June, John Burgess (Yamaha) set a new lap record for the revised circuit in 1m10.42s, 94.57mph

To general relief, the circuit changes had slowed the speeds markedly but had done nothing to harm the popularity of Castle Combe. If anything, fans now had two new viewing opportunities and drivers faced a fresh challenge. As the 50th anniversary approached, the circuit was proving more popular than ever.

Chapter 9

More than
just
a race circuit

While the major headlines from the 50-year history of Castle Combe centre around race action on both two and four wheels, the circuit has played host to a wide array of motorsport activity over those five decades. From small club events to a stage of a round of the World Rally Championship, the circuit has been used for every conceivable type of event.

Even in the year that the circuit opened, non-racing events were organised and it was the Bristol Motor Cycle and Light Car Club Mendip Petit Prix that was the first non-racing event to make use of the Wiltshire track. The full title of this unique event was the Mendip Petit Prix de Tourisme and it is remembered with great enthusiasm by many.

The Mendip Grand Prix was an idea of Dick Caesar, who was an official of the Bristol club and creator of the Caesar Special and Iota racing cars. The event was first held in 1936 and is explained in the Bristol club's magazine of June 1954. 'It was originally run over a triangular course of about five miles on the Mendip Hills south of Bristol. At its inception Dick Caesar devised the event and it was intended to resemble a mock sports car race, but with the main emphasis on pit-work. It was intended that it remain suitable for the club member with his workaday car.'

The first event held at Castle Combe was on September 9 1950, and was won by John Buncombe in a 989cc Morris. Further Petits Prix were held at the circuit in the early 1950s and although other venues were used

after the club relinquished its lease on the circuit, Castle Combe was again used in 1958. Post-war events were run on the Mendips course in 1946 and 1947 on little used roads.

'This event has been allowed to lapse lately due to lack of support, which in turn was due to lack of petrol,' reported the Bristol club journal of June 1950. Petrol rationing had severely restricted non-essential motoring but the club was able to resurrect the event in 1950. In June 1954, the Bristol club explained the move to the airfield circuit. 'Three years ago it was decided to change the venue to Castle Combe, primarily because the public became very interested and it was feared that the B-class roads might become unduly congested. Though the police had always been co-operative it was considered undesirable to continue to use the area.'

In August 1951, an article in Autosport explained the rules. 'Briefly, the plot requires a set distance at a comparatively low average speed but the main object is to carry out about a dozen detailed pit-stops during the event. The pit-stops include plug replacement, wheel-changing and taking on a couple of gallons of petrol, all these operations being stop-watch timed. The lowest aggregate times together with the maintenance of the set average speed decides the winner. Any type of car is eligible and a Le Mans-type start is used. Over the years a multitude of time-saving devices has been evolved, though freak appliances, such as the normal house tap once introduced by a competitor for radiator drainage, are discouraged. Up to last year it carried the title Grand

Prix, but in deference to the RAC, who felt that the term abused the grande epreuve designation, it was accordingly reduced in stature.'

Pit-stops were timed from crossing a line on the entry to the pits, to crossing a line on the exit. Each car carried two people and only they were permitted to work on the car in the pits. Pit tests included such devious exercises as removing and replacing one quart of water from the radiator and removing the rotor arm, throwing it into a can of water provided and replacing it. 'The event is amusing for the spectators, especially the sight of competitors dealing with hot engine parts in a great hurry,' said one contemporary report.

Brian Owens was a local lad when the early road events were run. 'When I was a youngster, just before the war, my father took me up to see the original one, which was run on public roads in the Mendips. That was great fun. Just a triangular circuit of lanes, and all these cars flying around. Nobody seemed to mind. After the war at Castle Combe three of us ran as a team, myself with the Frazer Nash, a friend with a 3-litre Bentley and another friend, Roy Spiers with an Alfa Romeo. We won the team award. People doing the jobs in the pits were changing plugs, draining the water out and losing it all before they'd had time to put it all back in again. Roy Spiers didn't switch the engine off when his mechanic tried to change the plugs, which was quite a sight. The air was blue.' The Autosport report of that September 1951 event, won by J Earle Marsh in a 4.5-litre Invicta, recalled the moment. 'Considerable amusement was caused at the plug-changing pit when a certain competitor tried to start his engine while his mechanic was still tightening up two plugs. The latter's shouts were clearly audible several pits down the line!'

In 1951 and 1952, Castle Combe played host to the Hants & Berks Motor Club Versatility Trial. It was conceived by Joe Lowrey, of the Hants and Berks club who was also technical editor of Motor magazine. 'I suggested an event in which the good all-purpose car could shine. It was to be a three part event. A morning speed event on a road racing track, an afternoon trial on difficult hills during which lowered tyre pressure would be forbidden, and judging on practical amenities of the

car. Not owning a circuit, we had to seek the help of another club. The Bristol MC&LCC provided Castle Combe, conveniently close to Cotswolds trials hills. The first event was staged in April 1951 attracting 39 entries. Three laps of the circuit, with cars run against the clock in batches of six, eliminated some fancied Dellows, pistons in their supercharged Ford 10 engines failing to stand the heat.'

For 1952 the laps of the circuit were changed slightly. 'A timed test, from a standing start to a flying finish over three laps of the circuit augmented by the introduction of two chicanes. As a tie decider a special test was then held which was a wiggle-woggle over some 100 yards of track before finishing by reversing into a garage,' said an Autosport report in May. The best time in the speed test was set by Derek Buckler (Buckler), but Nancy Mitchell (HRG) won the event overall. That was its final year at Castle Combe and it ran for the third and final time in 1953 when it used the Ibsley circuit.

In March 1952, the Circuit hosted a visit from the RAC International Rally of Great Britain. The event covered 1800 miles but this was more than 10 years before the rally headed into the forests for special stages. A timed test organised by Bristol MC&LCC awaited the competitors after which the cars headed into Wales. 'At Castle Combe a special test was held on the race track in the dark. Starting when a red control light changed to green, competitors had to accelerate forwards into a bay 30 yards ahead on their left and marked by a single overhead light. They then reversed out and continued into a similar and parallel bay 33 yards further on, and so out forwards to a flying finish over a line another 30 yards on. It was close to freezing point and the road bore ice patches in places,' said the Autosport report. The fastest times were set by Ken Bancroft (Morgan) and Teddy Booth (Jowett Jupiter).

A similar test was held on the same event in 1953 on the first night of the five-day rally and again in 1956. In early May 1953, the BARC South Western centre organised the North Devon Rally which featured a 500 mile road section. The first special test was a two-lap regularity test in the dark at Castle Combe. More events of this nature followed in 1955 with a Brighton and Hove

Motor Club rally in March and the Bugatti Owners' Club Winter Rally in December. All the tests were held at Castle Combe on Saturday afternoon, followed by road sections on Sunday.

The tests included a five-lap speed test, of which the fastest lap counted and an acceleration and braking test in the paddock area. Next came a one-hour high-speed trial, with the fastest cars set to do 40 laps, averaging over 73mph on a damp surface. The entry was divided into three sections for the high-speed trial, each group having an hour to itself. Fastest was Tommy Sopwith in a Cooper-Jaguar. 'Sydney Allard had quite a moment when a half shaft of his blue Ford Zephyr became semi-detached and he shot off into the infield minus brakes and gears. He screwed it all together again and rejoined the fray,' said the Motor report of the event. Just one Bugatti entered, a T57S coupe and Mike Hawthorn watched it all as event steward.

More traditional competitive events were the sprints held at the circuit. Although the circuit had been used for racing from 1950, it was not until car racing took a temporary enforced break that sprinting began. The first sprint was run by the Bristol club in May 1956 over a standing start quarter mile. Fastest time of the day went to John Buncombe (Tojeiro Bristol) in 16.2s while Henry Liddon (Standard) was second in the up to 1000cc saloons and first in the 1300-1800cc saloons with an MG. Liddon would go on be a Monte Carlo Rally winning co-driver and Toyota rally team manager.

Over the following years, several similar events were held and from 1960 to 1963 the Dursley Motor Cycle and Light Car Club also used the venue. The course for this event used the section of track from Tower to Quarry and fastest time went to Wally Cuff (1100cc Cooper-JAP) in 56.72s. Bath garage owner, and later frequent race winner at the circuit, Ron Fry was second in the 1600cc saloon class in a Riley and first in the over 1600cc saloon class in an Aston Martin.

Karting was an emerging sport in the 1960s and the Bath Karting Club was responsible for the introduction of karting to Castle Combe. Initially the track was around the roads of the paddock. Later, it also used parts of the finishing straight from the paddock entrance to the control tower, marked with straw bales. Mrs Thomas gave the club permission to resurface the perimeter track of the paddock for the kart track as well.

In 1960, the Bath KC National Championship meeting was held on September 24 and comprised 15 races, culminating in a two-driver 100-lap race which qualified for a national championship on a 1000-yard course. The following year, the club ran meetings on a 900-yard paddock circuit and in 1961 Dorset racer Jim Fiander proved the hero of the day. 'Despite being flung from his machine when his steering butterfly sheared off, the Blandford Forum driver, Jim Fiander, dragged his McCulloch-powered Progress over the finishing line to collect points for seventh place during an eliminator for the British RAC kart championships. Careering off the track his machine hit the stout wooden palings and flung him wide. Although badly shaken he suffered only cut and bruises and insisted on finishing on foot,' said the Karting magazine report of the meeting.

The following year an Easter Monday kart meeting attracted 2500 spectators while a meeting in May included rising stars Roger Keele, Roy James and Chris Lambert in the entry. Uniquely for Castle Combe, karting also produced a Boxing Day event in 1964 when Lambert won twice as did John Greasley from Minehead. At Easter 1965 the circuit hosted its biggest kart meeting when the Bath Kart Club organised the Gallahers International Kart Meeting. The weekend featured practice on Friday, Saturday races on the full circuit, and Easter Monday races on a half-mile paddock circuit when 6,000 spectators were reported.

On Saturday Class Four events on the full circuit drew 90 entries including five Italians, one Swiss and one Dutch driver. In the Super final, Chris Lambert won and set a fastest lap at over 77mph. On Monday there were 165 entries for the International event, including a team of Italians using works Parilla engines led by Guido Sala. Unbeknown at the time, this was just about the end of karting at the circuit and by 1967 the Bath club had switched its meetings to the Clay Pigeon track in Dorset.

'Karting in its unsilenced form had badly damaged local relations and we paid the price for decades to come,' relates Strawford.

Sprints continued to be a regular part of the Castle Combe calendar, even when car racing was temporarily halted. Through the 1960s, at least three sprints were held each year and in some seasons as many as eight. 1965 appears to have been the busiest year ever for the circuit with eight sprints, 11 car race meetings, four motor-cycle race meetings and a kart meeting on the full circuit, giving a total of 24 meetings. This included a sprint held on Sunday 18 July, the day after a 750 MC race meeting. This seems sure to have been the only event run on a Sunday until the 1990s. However, a finish deadline of 5.45pm meant that not everyone was able to take their second runs according to reports of the event.

Many variations of course were used over the years, with different organising clubs each having their own ideas. The courses ranged from standing start quarter mile right through to three lap runs. The most unusual was the Dursley MC 'round the barrel' layout used in 1961 and 1962. 'The course was exactly one mile in length, starting on Dean Straight then using Camp Corner and all the road in front of the paddock. It ran away to the left of the paddock to a point 880 yards from the start where a barrel was placed in the middle of the track and around which the competitors turned. The course then ran back the way it had come to the finish. The Lister Jaguar of Ken Wilson had to proceed over 150 yards past the barrel to find a piece of road wide enough to turn. Then he had to use the grass as he had very little lock,' said the Autosport report of the August 1962 event.

The multi-lap sprints were generally run as pursuit sprints, with four cars on the track at once started at intervals. By the late 1960s the two-lap sprint appeared to become the standard format and these events sometimes attracted surprisingly large crowds, with well over 1000 spectators reported at a BARC event in April 1964. On occasions, the crowds were well entertained as the Motoring News report of a Burnham-on-Sea Motor Club Sprint in July 1966 records.

'Ian Perrett (Lotus Cortina) caught up to within 25 yards of Dave Harris (Willment Cortina GT) from the standing start and then on the flyer they came into Camp separated by only ten yards. Harris took all the road and Perrett took all that and two yards of grass verge. Ian Swift appeared with his Swift-Ford 4.7 single-seater hillclimb car determined to capture fastest time of the day. On the flying lap of his first run the big car screamed through Camp Corner, the tail slid wildly at the exit, it rotated through about 270 degrees, shot off backwards for 50 yards into the hay field and came gently to rest against some freshly stacked straw bales! During this process it had crossed the finish line backwards and a time of 2min 24.2s was registered although it didn't count because he was off the track. On his second run he posted a rather more subdued 2m 29.2s.'

Many drivers who went on to great success in racing, initially started in sprinting and amongst the regular competitors at Castle Combe at the time were Vince Woodman, Geoff Mabbs, Brian Cutting, Jan Odor, Jonathan Buncombe, Richard Longman and Jeremy Lord. Ron Fry scored many fastest times with his Aston Martin DB4, before competing with a succession of Ferraris and Ford GT40s, often entering his Downton Mini-Cooper as well. Frequently, he debuted his latest acquisition in a sprint before racing it for the first time.

However, as the planning problems really took hold of the circuit, sprints were one of the casualties and the final events of the era were held in 1970. Then, as severe restrictions were placed on Castle Combe's sporting events, it would be 11 years before speed events made a brief return. At short notice in 1981, the Welsh Counties Car Club filled a spare race-day freed up by a successful planning enquiry with a one and three-quarter lap sprint on October 31.

In both 1974 and 1976 the Tour of Britain visited Castle Combe for a series of races, but it was in November 1983 that the Lombard RAC Rally brought world class rally action to the circuit. It was one of the years that the rally was based in Bath and the Castle Combe stage was the third of the opening day, after stages at Longleat and Ashton Court, as the cars competed over a series of spectator stages in the south west. From the start in the paddock, it followed a very twisty route around the paddock roads, past the scrutineering bay, turned right under the Avon Bridge to go the wrong way up the pit entry road. The stage then turned hairpin left onto the circuit and then followed the lap to finish just before Westway.

Fastest time on the stage was set by the Audi Quattro of Hannu Mikkola/Arne Hertz in 1m 48s from the similar car of Stig Blomqvist/ Bjorn Cederberg (1m 49s). Three cars tied on 1m50s with the Toyota Celica of Per Eklund, co-driven by Dave Whittock from Bath, the Audi Quattro of Michele Mouton/Fabrizia Pons and the Toyota Celica of Bjorn Waldegard/Hans Thorszelius. Blomqvist/Cederberg went on to win the event and hosting the rally provided an unexpected bonus for the circuit. 'Totally unbeknown to me, getting planning permission for that created a precedent so we then asked for permission to run the Norwich Union Classic Run from here. We've run that ever since and have also run other classic events as a result,' says Howard Strawford.

A largely unsuccessful attempt to revive the Tour of Britain resulted in the 1989 Autoglass Tour. Only around 30 cars entered the event and it visited Castle Combe on a weekday for a 16-lap race in which Jimmy McRae (Ford RS Sierra Cosworth) set the pace. More popular, however, were the RAC Historic Rallies of the early 1990s. In March 1991 the first RAC Historic Rally featured a mix of regularity sections and timed tests, including a stage at Castle Combe. 'The start was in the paddock, the route then flicking round the perimeter roads before hitting the circuit proper. The lap which followed involved three truly evil chicanes, which saw one or two of the bigger cars having to take two or three bites,' said the Autosport report. The fastest time on this stage was set by rally legend Rauno Aaltonen in a Mini-Cooper. The following year the event had become a proper stage rally under the title of the Charringtons RAC International Historic Rally and, on the second day of rally, the circuit hosted two stages, each comprising two laps of the circuit. Five years on, the 1997 RAC International Historic Rally ran in tandem with the Network Q Rally of Great Britain from a Cirencester

base. A pursuit sprint at Castle Combe completed the first day of the rally.

Aside from the single event in 1981, sprints had been absent from Castle Combe for 20 years such was the constraint of planning permission. The Bristol Aeroplane Company Motor Club had been co-promoting sprints at the MoD Colerne airfield since 1978, only about 15 minutes away from Castle Combe. However, in the mid-1980s the use of Colerne was being threatened by increased security precautions in the face of terrorist activity and so the club was looking for alternative sprint venues. The club had also been running a day for its members at Castle Combe for some time, within the limitations of silenced road car use. However, use of the circuit for a sprint had always appeared to be ruled out by the limited number of noisy race days permitted.

In 1990 the club's vice-chairman Pete Stowe recognised that there were enough sprint competitors around whose cars complied with the lower road car noise limit of 102 dB(a) instead of the normal sprint limit of 113 dB(a), that a quiet sprint ought to be possible. Howard Strawford was approached with the proposal and was supportive, which resulted in temporary planning permission for a trial event. With sponsorship from Steven Roberts at Merlin Motorsports, 99 quiet cars took part in the first Pegasus Sprint on October 26 1991. Fastest time of the day went to Tony Michael (Westfield) on the three-quarter lap course from the startline to Westway.

Following this successful trial meeting permanent planning permission was then granted, and the Bristol Motor Cycle and Light Car Club joined in with a second event, returning to the venue that the club had created back in 1950. The BAC MC event was extended to use the full lap in 1995, and in 1998 represented the final competitive event to be held on the original track, before the new corners were introduced. Geoff Kershaw set fastest time of the day in his Turbo Technics Ford Sierra as the event brought to a conclusion the 48 year history of the original circuit layout.

The modern day kart track and skid pan behind Old Paddock.

Classic car runs and rallies are regular visitors to the circuit.

Photo: John Gaisford.

Chapter 10

The medical team

Over the 50-year history of Castle Combe, medical facilities at race circuits have changed beyond all recognition. In the early years, medical cover was scant to say the least but has since developed into a highly organised and immensely professional aspect of the modern sport. Progress at the Wiltshire track has mirrored that development and is in no small way due to the dedication, enthusiasm and expertise of the circuit's medical team. For 30 years, that team was led by Dr Peter Baskett.

'I was actually first involved in motor racing medicine in the 1950s,' recalls Baskett. 'I was a medical student in Belfast and used to go to a circuit called Dundrod, which held the Ulster Tourist Trophy. The race had my heroes racing, one of which was Stirling Moss. Juan-Manuel Fangio, Peter Collins and Tony Brooks all used to race on that road circuit which was a hugely dangerous place with stone walls and telegraph poles. They were absolutely brilliant, but in those days they had hardly any doctors. I went along and offered my services as a medical student and stood on a corner with a bag and a few bits and pieces. In those days, knowledge of the airway was limited and things like mouth to mouth and chest compressions were only just coming in.'

His enthusiasm for motor cars took Baskett into competition at club level, but it was to be his part in motorsport medical services that would occupy much of his working career. 'I had raced a little bit myself at Kirkistown and did a bit of rallying as well so I knew about the sport. When I came over to England in 1963 I got involved again at Castle Combe, my local circuit. There was a chief medical officer at that time and I worked with him. There was a medical room with a couch in it, but we had very little equipment. He carried his doctor's bag and, being an anaesthetist at the time, I tended to bring all the stuff I could carry for resuscitation. I was only a registrar at the time, so I hadn't got much equipment.'

By the time the existing chief medical officer stood down, Howard Strawford had taken a key role in running race meetings at the circuit for the BRSCC and was quick to encourage Baskett to take over the role. 'In 1968 Howard asked me to be chief medical officer and I brought some colleagues with me. I was working at Frenchay Hospital in Bristol and by now was a consultant there. We gradually built up a team of about a dozen doctors. We also built up the equipment we had,' he says.

However, the parlous state of circuit finances at the start of the 1970s meant that Castle Combe was always stretched to provide facilities, when simply keeping the circuit open was a major problem.

'Eventually we acquired a rescue vehicle and the Roger Williamson Fund helped us with equipment. David Nancekevill at Brands Hatch was quite a pioneer for the rescue unit and the doctors' car and I worked with him quite a lot. I picked up a lot of ideas from him and Brands was richer in those days than Castle Combe and could afford more equipment,' recalls Baskett.

The circuit's medical team poses outside the medical centre.

However, despite limited financial resources, Castle Combe's doctors were among the most experienced in the country and Baskett was determined to develop the team. 'In the 1970s I had become a regular doctor at the Grand Prix at both Brands and Silverstone and the thing then was to wear overalls. I got people to buy blue overalls for Castle Combe and we were slightly ridiculed because we were thought of as posers in uniforms, but I held out and since then it has become obligatory. Prior to that, doctors at race meetings wore sheepskin coats!'

As the sport progressed into the 1980s, everything around running and organising the sport became more professional and so the requirements for medical facilities laid down by the sport's governing body became more exacting. One of the familiar features of Castle Combe meetings for more than a decade has been the fast intervention vehicle, crewed by medical officers and veteran racer Terry Sanger.

'We borrowed a fast car from Brown Brothers to chase the pack around the first lap. Then we acquired our own car though the courtesy of Honda, which had some prototype cars that were not road legal, but were ideal for use on the circuit,' says Baskett. The doctor's car ensures that medical assistance can be on the scene of a first-lap incident within seconds and is constantly on stand-by throughout the rest of the race. Thankfully rarely needed, it is nevertheless a key element in providing swift response to any incident.

'At the end of the 1993 season the medical centre was extended and we built a resuscitation area which is well equipped with all the kit you could need. Before that there was only one room for patients,' says Baskett.

The calibre of medical officer on duty at Castle Combe is among the very highest of any circuit in Britain. 'Castle Combe now produces about a third of the doctors for the British Grand Prix. We've got some pretty class acts amongst our team,' says Baskett. 'We have now built up a team covering various specialities including plastic surgeons, general practitioners and mostly anaesthetists along with paramedics and nurses. We don't get paid for what we do. If we had demanded pay in accordance with what doctors earn, the circuit would not have been able to afford it. So we always had as many doctors as possible and as a gesture from the club, we all go out to dinner once a year. Most circuits pay their doctors, but we take it that we don't get paid and we do it for the love of the sport. They wouldn't be there if they didn't enjoy motorsport.'

It is not just the competitors, however, who call on the medical services during race meetings. 'Members of the crowd represent a very large proportion of the people we see at a race meeting. It is really like being a GP in a small town for the day and a lot of things we see is general practice stuff, especially over a Bank Holiday meeting. We do the best we can and try and help people. The majority of stuff is trivial to us as doctors, but not to the patient. Wasp stings are very common, so are bits of things in eyes. They're not life threatening, but can be pretty inconvenient to the patient.

'We've had a number of heart attacks at race meetings. We have revived several people after cardiac arrests. One particular person, who was the father of a racing driver, had an arrest twice at different race meetings, which was very unusual. Both times he survived when we resuscitated him. He got better from the first one and then did it again the next year. For a father, watching his son racing can be very stressful.

Having completed 30 years as chief medical officer, Baskett decided to take a step back towards the end of the 1990s. 'I wanted to let the younger guys develop. In 1997, Gerry Nolan took over as chief and I now act as his deputy. I still enjoy doing it, but I wanted to hand over to a younger chap and he is doing very, very well and also brings in new doctors. At some meetings we can have 15 or 16 doctors on hand, although the MSA minimum requirement is only two. We always have at least six doctors,' says Baskett.

Apart from their obvious enthusiasm for the sport, doctors can benefit in terms of learning from working at a race meeting. 'You can learn a huge amount. You learn a certain skill that I call working out of a box. In hospital

Most incidents, like this MG Midget drama at Quarry, do not result in injury.

Photo: Steve Jones.

Keith Macaskill pressing on before his terrible accident in August 1996.

practice now, a lot of doctors have never worked at the scene of an accident and don't know what equipment they will need. We have learned that you don't burden yourself like a packhorse. We have refined it down to a very simple little bag which is life saving and the rest of the stuff comes in the ambulance. The bag is what we have for the doctor on the corner and we normally have a doctor at Quarry, Tower and Camp at the very least during race meetings,' says Baskett.

'This also gives people experience in watching it happen, which is a very different thing to seeing a person even a few minutes later. When you see an almighty crash and someone ploughing into the barriers, there is bound to be an element of adrenaline in yourself. You learn to discipline yourself not to rush straight in, but weigh up the risks and that is very applicable to the management of a major incident like a train crash or aeroplane accident for example.

'You also see different aspects of patients' symptoms. The classic thing in a person with a serious head injury who may well suffer permanent injury is two large pupils. That is usually a sign that the person has had a major head injury. Now we see that quite commonly in the first two to three minutes after the accident when the pupils can be enormous. In fact, that is concussion which is very transient and after three or four minutes they come round and the pupils come down in size. That is something that I have learnt over the years, that you can see signs that could be initially confusing because you have been there almost too early. We actually watch it happen, which is very good experience. I have been able to write this up and talk about it during lectures.

'Doctors also learn basic skills like how to splint people and how to get them out of cars, which is normally done by ambulance crews. We can now appreciate what the ambulance crews have to contend with,' says Baskett.

Over the years there have been many major incidents resulting in a wide range of injuries. Few have been serious, but one stands out in recent history that tested the Castle Combe medical team to the full. The August Bank Holiday Monday meeting in 1996 featured several sizeable accidents, but it was in the immediate aftermath of the shunt on the opening lap of the Handygas Saloon Car race that the team really showed its expertise.

Hard-charging Scot Keith Macaskill's Vauxhall Astra spun on the exit of Old Paddock and was t-boned with terrifying force by, ironically, the Nova of team-mate Warren Dunbar. The impact was on the driver's side of Macaskill's car and he suffered terrible injuries as a result. Dunbar was also injured, but to a lesser extent. There is no doubt that the swift and decisive action by the doctors on duty saved Macaskill's life and ensured he went on to make a fine recovery.

'Keith Macaskill is our great pride and joy,' says Baskett. 'We're very proud of Keith because he had terrible injuries with a major fracture of the pelvis and he's lucky to be alive. He was very, very badly hurt but did remarkably well. We stabilised his pelvis at the circuit, otherwise he would have bled to death. That saved him initially and then he received very good treatment in Frenchay Hospital in Bristol. Many of us on duty that day were working at Frenchay, so we saw him the next day. He has been so appreciative and has been back to see us. He has been so keen to say thank you and we have a plaque from him in the medical centre.'

However, not all those on the receiving end of medical treatment are as appreciative as Macaskill. 'We've had some amazingly stupid drivers over the years, who have got quite cross and come in blaming the other guy and blaming the doctors for his accident,' says Baskett. 'You have to take a fairly firm line at times like that. The nicest

Graham Presley escaped unharmed from this fiery accident at Old Paddock in 1997.

guys to treat are the motorcycle racers. They are superb guys who fall off and can get terribly painful injuries by sliding on their backsides or breaking legs and collarbones. Generally speaking, their attitude is to check on the well-being of the other rider first, whereas some of the racing drivers come in ranting about the other driver. Part of the art of doctoring is being a nice chap but fairly firm.'

Throughout the years, one person has been a regular caller to the Castle Combe medical centre. 'We treat Howard at every meeting,' reckons Baskett. 'He always has some ailment. You see him first thing in the morning and he usually says, 'glad you're here, dear boy!' Howard is allegedly very careful with money but he has been very, very supportive of me over the years. Anything I have wanted in terms of equipment, I've not always got the first time, but I've got it in the end.'

Chapter 11

Local heroes
by
Dud Candler

Formula Ford 1600 Championship

Circuit-based championships play a major role in the Castle Combe story, and traditionally form the core of every meeting. From Formula Ford 1600s to the sports-racers in the Special GT championship to the more recent saloon car series, the leading drivers are true local heroes thanks to the large and enthusiastic crowds that line the circuit.

The Formula Ford 1600 series lays rightful claim to be Britain's oldest regional FF1600 series. First held in

Bryan Sharp on his way to the very first Castle Combe Formula Ford title.

Photo: Ferret Fotographics.

John Moon interviews four-times champion Bob Higgins.

1969, it pre-empted the Champion of Brands series by a year. While that first championship, won by Merlyn Mk11 driver Bryan Sharp, was unsponsored, Guards cigarettes came in the next year. Guards was the first of many sponsors, later to include the Ross and Haines garage business along with its associated night-club Goldiggers, Ford dealer Earle of Chippenham, Square Grip and HEAT (the Heat Electric Advisory Team).

Early FF1600 visitors included the Frank Williams Racing Team, later to become Williams Grand Prix Engineering, with American driver John Bisignano, as well as future multiple British Touring Car champion Andy Rouse who cut his racing teeth in a Dulon LD4C. How many fans in the crowd on September 11 1976 realised that they were witnessing a future British world champion in FF1600 race winner Nigel Mansell? The 1978 season was another landmark in Castle Combe history. With the closure of the Llandow circuit in South Wales, the FF1600 and Special Saloon Car

championships became one circuit series. Prior to that, both had been known as BRSCC South West series, featuring rounds at both circuits. Indeed, in its early years, the FF1600 championship had also taken in races at Thruxton.

By its very position, Castle Combe has always attracted a strong following from West Country drivers as well as a number from across the Severn bridge. Few champions have bucked that trend, although American Buzz Buzaglo who won the 1972 title in an Elden Mk10 is one notable exception.

However, in the circuit's 50-year history, few drivers have been as consistently successful as quadruple champions Bob Higgins and Gavin Wills. Both have records that stand close scrutiny, for with a little more luck, either could have added a fifth or perhaps even a sixth title. Higgins had raced at Castle Combe for several years before taking his first title in 1981. That he

Long-standing circuit commentator Richard Davies interviews Formula Ford heroes Gavin Wills (centre) and Kevin Mills (right).

achieved it in an unfashionable Martlet chassis served only to further his reputation. He retained his crown the following year but switched to a Royale RP29A to make it three on the trot in 1983. All the while, the Bath taxi driver was existing on a minuscule budget. He would go on to take a fourth title, albeit some eleven years after his first. A tenacious spirit allied to his outgoing personality and rich West Country accent made him a really firm favourite with the crowds.

Gavin Wills was a fresh faced youngster when he arrived on the scene in 1988. Few outside karting knew much about him, but he was soon putting the regulars in their place. Despite starting the season late, he wrapped up the title in some style. He retained his crown in 1989, although not without drama. Going to the finale, he trailed Higgins and David Davies. Both his rivals went off in separate incidents at Camp corner, giving Wills a

clear run to the title. The rapid, but erratic, Davies lost not only the title, but also his racing licence for 30 days after physically assaulting fellow driver Steve Deeks, who was still strapped in his car following their crash!

Although Wills later branched out onto the national scene, a move that eventually led to him purchasing the ailing Swift racing car marque, he was destined to return to Castle Combe where he added back to back titles in 1993 and 1994 driving a Swift SC92F.

Variety in winning chassis was a strong feature of the early years of the championship. Although the all-conquering Van Diemen marque arrived on the scene as early as 1973, surprisingly the Norfolk manufacturer had to wait until 1986 to claim a Castle Combe title, when Robert Davies took the crown back to Tenby.

So, who were the early heroes? Following Bryan Sharp's inaugural crown, Peter Lamplough gave the Palliser marque its only Castle Combe title in 1970. Mike Campbell-Cole raced his Merlyn to the crown in 1971, while Terry Richards was the last Merlyn driver to lift a Castle Combe title when he won it in 1975. Most notably of this trio, Campbell-Cole returned to racing and winning titles in the late 1990s, after a quarter of a century away.

Clive Power and Roger Orgee won back to back titles with the same Dulon MP15 in 1973 and 1974, when Orgee bought the car from Power for the 1974 season. The MP15 was almost certainly the best model from a marque that had started life building 750 and 1172 Formula cars. Power, a local dentist, later became involved in a press capacity at the circuit, while Orgee went on to race a variety of cars before moving into team management.

Elden enjoyed a solitary title via Buzz Buzaglo in 1972, while the Irish Crossle marque took its only Castle Combe crown when Surrey driver Geoff Davies raced successfully in the ex-Colin Lees 32F in 1979. The rare Jomic chassis also made its mark in the hands of John Peters and Mike Wallaker. In 1977, Peters led the championship prior to the double points finale, but crashed in qualifying. Although he got the car fit to race, he couldn't prevent the Royale RP21-mounted David Wheeler from taking the title. Having contested an early season race and scored well, Cambridgeshire racer Wheeler decided to carry on contesting the championship and finally clinched the title in one of the classic RP21 chassis.

Wallaker avenged Peters' defeat by going one better in 1978. It was a close run thing with just one point separating Wallaker and Wheeler. Although Wheeler never won in Wiltshire again, Castle Combe was a happy hunting ground for Royale drivers. Welshman David Toye took the crown in an RP21 in 1976, while the penniless, but highly talented, Steve Lincoln from Bristol took the 1980 title in his RP26. Bob Higgins, in 1983, and Martin Cooper, who'd got his 1984 title-winning campaign underway at the wheel of an RP33M, added further to the marque's tally.

There is more than a touch of irony that David Llewellyn who was one of Royale's longest and most loyal customers, should finally achieve his long held ambition of taking the title in 1987, but in a Van Diemen. The popular Welshman had run a string of Royales, but by 1987 the firm founded by Bob King had ceased trading!

Martin Cooper has a place in the record books as the only Castle Combe champion to use two different makes of chassis in a title winning year. Having started out 1984 in one of the largely unsuccessful Royale RP33Ms, he then switched to a Reynard 83/84FF, which at the time was very much the chassis to have. Cooper's switch was prompted by the fact that major rival Howard Lester was already in one of the Bicester built cars and was proving a tough nut to crack. Lester was something of an enigma, for although he was very quick and would win the title easily a year later, he rarely went well when he ventured away from Castle Combe.

Together with brother Alan, Martin Cooper went on to found the Formula Ford marque bearing the family name. However, Martin later became disillusioned and quit the sport, while Alan became central to the running of the circuit's race school days and in 1999 took over ownership of the Swift marque from Gavin Wills.

Following Lester's 1985 title, it would be another five years before a Reynard driver got his hands on a Castle Combe title. This was Welshman Nigel Jenkins who scooped successive titles in 1990 and 1991. In the latter year, he held off a challenge from Ian McArdell who had already tasted success having lifted the Champion of Snetterton Formula Ford title in 1989. McArdell's efforts earned him BRSCC South West Driver of the Year award in 1991. Although he enjoyed that, Ian so wanted to win the Castle Combe crown. Just when it seemed that his dream was about to come true, tragedy struck. After a season-long battle with Bob Higgins in 1992, he led by three points going into the final round. That morning in the paddock he spoke of the need to be just behind his rival to take the title. Come the afternoon, the racing driver's will to win took over. Trying to defend his spot, the duo touched on the run to Old Paddock. Ian's car turned left and slammed into the barrier at unabated pace. The chassis stood up well but poor Ian sustained severe

Ian McArdell leads the Formula Ford pack as others hit drama.

Photo: Steve Jones

Bob Higgins salutes the crowd after another victory.

Photo: Steve Jones

A typical Formula Ford pack heads for Old Paddock.

Photo: Steve Jones.

head injuries and died in Bristol's Frenchay Hospital on Monday afternoon. It was a devastating blow to everyone involved in the championship and Ian's family would later make a substantial donation towards expansion of the circuit's medical facilities.

When Gavin Wills lifted his third title in 1993, it was a first Castle Combe crown for the Swift marque. Wills won again in 1994 in a period that saw Swift drivers lifting titles in five successive seasons. In fact a Swift had raced at the circuit many years earlier, but it had nothing to do with the better known marque. This was the self-built machine of local farmer Ian Moore. He was something of a circuit hero during the 1970s while his son, Ed, would also become a Castle Combe favourite in the nineties.

By the midway point of the decade, the ascendancy of Kevin Mills was opening another chapter of the championship's history. Mills had first raced at the circuit in 1994 in a six year-old Van Diemen. The efforts of the personable Gloucester racer had been noticed, as he was often just behind the established regulars.

Armed with a Swift SC92F for the 1995 season, Mills was now on an equal footing and able to do battle with Gavin Wills. Similarity of their names resulted in their battles being dubbed 'the Mills and Wills show'. A play on words was fine for the written press, but not so good for race commentators who had much less time to say the right name. To ensure the task wasn't made any easier, both drove cars which were predominantly white.

The Mills and Wills show ran and ran, with Mills finally emerging ahead by a solitary point in 1995. Mills retained his crown by a pretty comprehensive margin in 1996, when Wills did not compete. However, by season's end, the list of title challengers was growing. There was further interest in 1997, when a class for Pre '90 cars was added to the championship with support from racers John Hutchinson and Ian Riley through their Henley Sales Recruitment business. At the sharp end of the field, it was another classic, for although Mills bagged his hat-trick, the emerging Richard Carter ran him to equal points. Mills took the verdict on a tie break with the greater number of race wins but the Cornishman had shown his speed.

Things didn't always go smoothly for Robin Parsons. This is Camp Corner, 1995.

A few weeks later, Mills was just two laps away from adding the inaugural Formula Ford Carnival title to his CV when he spun off at Old Paddock. Carter, who'd driven the race of his life to come from the fifth row of the grid, gleefully grabbed his chance and held off Gavin Wills to win by just a fifth of a second. The Carnival final was also notable in that Wills finally broke Marc Goossens' lap record that had stood for seven years. His new mark would stand throughout the following season and so ensure him a place in the record books as the circuit layout changed for 1999.

By the end of 1997 Kevin Mills had completely emptied his budget and stood down from racing in 1998, preferring to prepare cars for other drivers in the hope that he would one day get back behind the wheel himself. While he looked on, Carter won the championship after a fine season-long tussle with Salisbury farmer Robin Parsons.

Just as a year earlier, the champion would be denied the honours at the Carnival. Those fell to Parsons who would go on to win the season opener the following year

on the revised circuit. Try as he may, Parsons couldn't wrest the championship crown from Carter, but in an action replay of a year earlier, Parsons gained revenge on his conqueror at the Carnival. Blighted by the weather and shortened following earlier delays, the Carnival final brought down the curtain on the 20th century at Castle Combe. Formula Ford 1600 had been a central part of the track's history for thirty years and that will continue well into the new millennium.

Special GT and Saloon Championships

Castle Combe's other championships, for the ultra-quick Special GTs and Saloon Cars may not have such lengthy histories as their single-seater counterpart, but both enjoy strong support from both competitors and fans.

The Special GT series was first held in 1982, though its roots trace back to the circuit's own Special Saloon Car championship which ran from 1975 to 1981. The latter part of the 1970s was one of change within the category, not just at Castle Combe but at national level, as purpose-built spaceframe specials clothed in fibreglass took over from traditional modified cars using steel bodyshells. Another category suffering from declining numbers was Modified Sports. The answer was simple: combine them and then call it Special GT. Grids filled with such cars as Lotus Elans, Davrians and the nimble spaceframe Minis and Imps.

Over the years a number of drivers would become Castle Combe favourites, even though a major title was to evade them. Who will ever forget Fred Henderson and his seemingly fearless antics in his Chevrolet Camaro? Nobody before or since, has ever driven so many sideways laps of the Wiltshire circuit!

There was Bristol Ford dealer Vince Woodman and his truly superb Cologne Capri who had wowed the circuit regulars throughout the Thundersaloon era and then went on to enliven Special GT races. Lotus Elan racers Rob Cox, Andrew Wareing and Richard Ward all induced incredible pace out of their machines. Wareing ensured himself a place in the record books, when in

1984 he achieved a race average of 100.57mph, the first ever 100mph GT race at the track. The personable Ward, who later moved north but carried on racing, was a familiar sight with wife Barbara wheeling out the slave battery to start his car on the grid.

In the late 1980s and early 1990s, local man Dave Appleby showed that a Metro 6R4 could be a very quick car on the race tracks as well as in rally and rallycross circles. His pace and flamboyant style, developed on rally stages, made him an instant hero.

Castle Combe's first Special GT champion, Brian Cutting, was already a favourite with the crowds when he lifted the inaugural crown in 1982. The Bournemouth man had raced at the circuit for many years, twice winning the Special Saloon Car championship. Cutting used the same spaceframe Sunbeam Stiletto in which he'd taken the second of his Saloon Car titles. Always competitive, he often humbled much bigger engined cars. He added a further Special GT title in 1988, while his son Tony would also race at the circuit.

A GT pack at Old Paddock in the late 1980s.

Photo: Steve Jones.

The 1983 season was, sadly, notable for a quite horrible accident that befell the hugely popular Welshman Barry Reece. He'd raced a succession of highly-developed Minis before acquiring a really lightweight spaceframe Stiletto in which he had his career-ending accident. Following a brush with a rival in qualifying, the car slammed into the barriers and disintegrated. Its poor unprotected driver was exposed to an appalling catalogue of injuries. That year, Davrian driver Steven Roberts, who would go on to set up the circuit-based Merlin Motorsport, took the title in his Mini-engined Trans XL-backed car. Roberts dominated Class C, one of four classes in that era, to such an extent that his winning points total was almost double that of his nearest rival.

best race I ever had was a wet Castle Combe Special GT race against Peter Baldwin. There must have been a round of another championship for Peter to be here and he did the Castle Combe race as well. It was very wet for practice and the race and I'd had a good practice session and was on the front of the grid. He had a problem in practice and was in the middle of the grid. The rain was torrential in the race and I led him for 10 laps and we lapped everyone else. We still remember it. I was in the Davrian. If he got past, he would have disappeared, but because he was stuck in the pack at the start I got a couple of laps lee-way before he got onto my tail. It was magic. We both remember that race. I was jumped at the start by a Porsche and thought that if I didn't get past that soon I was going to park up because I couldn't see anything. But Peter started at the back and kept going, which is why he's so good.'

Brian Fisher's Skoda took the Special GT title in 1986 and 1987.

Photo: Steve Jones.

'I raced here first of all in 1973 and 1974. Then I started chasing national championships and I used to drive past the circuit on the way to Snetterton or Oulton Park or somewhere. I came back and did the local championships in 1983 and 1984,' says Roberts. 'The

Roberts launched a successful title defence in 1984, although this time his winning margin wasn't quite so big. Sussex man Robin Harvey continued Davrian's winning streak a year later and was unlucky not to lift back-to-back titles in 1986. Harvey carried a two point

Bob Light heads the Special GT pack into Quarry.

Photo: Steve Jones.

lead to the final round, but his Imp-engined car broke its camshaft while leading its class. The point for fastest lap wasn't enough to prevent Brian Fisher snatching the title by a solitary point. This was the first of the three Special GT titles for the Bridgwater hairdresser. Fisher used the same Richardson Ford-engined Skoda clone to retain his crown in 1987. He went for the hat-trick the following year, which proved a cracker, but just lost out to Brian Cutting who clinched a second Special GT crown.

George Douglas and Nigel Mustill fought out the championship's closest ever finish in 1989, the duo inseparable after every tie-break rule had been applied. Douglas drove a rare Ginetta G12, in which he still competes in historic events, while Mustill ran a potent Cosworth turbo-engined Ford Escort Mk1. A familiar figure at Castle Combe, Douglas supported the local championships via his Mobile Windscreens business. The following year, Salisbury commercial vehicle specialist Mustill retained his title, pipping Davrian racer Chris Snowdon by just one point.

Snowdon came out tops in 1991, but it was to be the final title won by a Modsports car. Major changes to regulations for the 1992 season saw the championship opened up to include the sports racing cars that became an integral part of the series in the second half of the 1990s. However, the open sports racers would have to wait three years before a title came along. Phil Lomas and then Erling Jensen were the men to deny them. Lomas took over the Tiga Sports 2000-based Skoda clone previously campaigned by his friend George Douglas to lift the crown in 1992. Jensen then bought the Rover V8-engined car from Douglas and went on to success in 1993, though the foundation for his title was laid in his Maguire Stiletto. It was a huge step up for the Bath based Dane who'd previously raced less powerful machines and his time with the Skoda was punctuated by a couple of hefty accidents.

Hard-charging Somerset racer Geoff Thorne lifted the title in 1994, although not without drama. His ex-Tony Wiltshire Lola T86/90 was blighted by a misfire, but kept going to hang on at the final round. Unwittingly, Thorne was also to play a part in the title outcome two years later. In between, Brian Fisher added a third title, although by now he was in a Ford BDA-engined Shrike P16. Fisher and title rival Chris Gilbert (Lola T87/90) caused a race stoppage in the final round when Gilbert collected a spinning Fisher. Neither man was able to take the re-start.

The 1996 outcome was even more curious, with Bob Light initially feted as champion after the final round. But he lost it half an hour later when a rival's car failed post-race scrutineering. Geoff Thorne had won Class C and taken the point for fastest lap, so denying fellow Class C man Keith Messer, the title. Thorne's car then failed a ride height test. His exclusion gave Messer the points to pip Light and John Robinson by one point! Although he'd been on the scene for a number of years, Light's sheer pace in his race-winning Chevrolet-engined Ultima had made him a crowd favourite. His B6 Sport, unveiled for the '99 season, further strengthened his claim.

While Light became the darling of Combe crowds, the mantle of Special GT champion for the final three years of the 1990s fell to Mallock Mk28 driver John Robinson. A good solid performer, the Guernseyman has never sought the spotlight. His on-track efforts, dominating Class B, have done the talking, earning him a spot in Combe folklore and his determination to race by commuting from Guernsey for each race has been well rewarded. The only other men to win three successive championship titles were Formula Ford aces Bob Higgins and Kevin Mills.

Although it was only inaugurated in 1995, the circuit's Saloon Car series quickly established itself as one of the most successful series in Britain. Howard Strawford and the team at the BRSCC recognised a need for a cost conscious series for road-going saloon cars in the West Country, and it was an instant hit when 44 competitors registered for the pilot races in 1995. Although certain modifications are allowed, the cars remain road-going type saloons and coupes. The fact that the cars run on road tyres rather than slicks, means that fans can truly equate them to the type of car they drive on the road.

Bottled and bulk tank gas supplier Handygas put its name to the series, and while that first season was non-points scoring, Keith Macaskill was deemed champion on theoretical scores. The new series soon threw up two new heroes in Macaskill and Ilsa Cox. Macaskill caught the attention of Castle Combe crowds with his intrepid handling of his 1600cc Vauxhall Nova in which he often beat much bigger engined rivals. He further endeared himself to regulars as each race required a 1200 mile round journey from his home in Aberdeen.

However, Macaskill was later badly hurt in August 1997, when he spun between Old Paddock and Tower and was heavily T-boned by Scottish team-mate Warren Dunbar. He remained a firm favourite with Castle Combe regulars and made a racing return at the circuit in April 2000.

Ilsa Cox got her name in the history books when she won the first ever Handygas race. Driving a Peugeot 205GTi prepared by husband Brian, himself a top Mini racer in the 1960s and 1970s, the Hove bank clerk and racing school instructor would go on to bigger things in 1997. Always willing to race hard against the men, Ilsa won the hearts of the crowd for her gritty performances.

While those two both became acclaimed series champions, others have made do with either class awards or simply becoming crowd favourites. Notable are Radstock's Julian Howell and his indecently quick Mini, John Moon (Vauxhall Nova and Calibra), Charles Atherton (Vauxhall Nova and Corsa) and former hillclimber Paul Brend who capped a highly memorable 1997 season with possibly the best ever drive in this championship.

Sussex man Derek Wileman became the first official champion when he lifted the crown in 1996. Wileman had raced a variety of saloon cars before campaigning a Vauxhall Cavalier GSi. The combination proved unstoppable, Wileman having the title in safe keeping before the final round. A year later, Ilsa Cox again ensured that the title went back to Sussex, albeit not without drama. She needed just one point from the final race of the season to be crowned champion. Only third fastest in practice, she set out to improve on that in the

Russell Humphrey and Brian Cox lead as the huge Pagid field heads for Old Paddock.
Photo: Steve Jones.

race. Battling for the lead with Class A rival Russell Humphrey (Vauxhall Astra), Ilsa spun off into the field on the inside of Folly. For a while it seemed that she might be stuck but finally the red Peugeot moved and she resumed, stone last. She tigered back to finish fourth overall and clinch the title. Although the title was now beyond him, Paul Brend enlivened the later race for Class B cars by overcoming a 10-second false start penalty and, driving as though his very life depended on it, went clear to win by some eight seconds!

A new series sponsor arrived for the 1998 season in the guise of Pagid Performance Braking, and once again

the title battle went to the wire. Vauxhall Astra GTE man Russell Humphrey emerged ahead, by dint of winning seven of the nine race series. Julian Howell proved his biggest threat, but Howell was himself facing stiff competition from Paul Gardner's Suzuki Swift and Charles Atherton's emerging Vauxhall Corsa. Howell, a former autograss racer, wowed the crowds with his on-the-limit driving style against the later machinery in the 1400cc class. While the three Class C men would prove extremely equally matched and so dilute points in the final championship of the millennium, it was left to racing returnee Brian Cox to become a major title contender along with Holt's Tim Hanlon. The Peugeot

Julian Howell, one of the stars of the Pagid series, in his giant-killing Mini.

Photo: Steve Jones.

205GTi mounted pair went head to head, albeit in different classes, but the month of August was to be the turning point. Cox's engine cut out when holding second spot at the first August meeting, but worse came at the Bank Holiday Monday meeting where he rolled at Quarry in qualifying after some form of transmission glitch. Hanlon needed no prompting to go on and grab the championship crown.

Packed grids and close racing from a wonderful array of cars had again proved that the Saloon Car Championship was a fine addition to the Formula Ford and Special GT Championships. No Castle Combe meeting would be complete without more action and drama from the local heroes.

Chapter 12

From little acorns

Now, 50 years on from the first meeting on the disused airfield, Castle Combe Circuit is a big business, contributing around £15 million to the local economy each year and providing pleasure, excitement and sport for thousands of enthusiasts. 'It's still very much a family business. When we took over the company it had a turnover of £15,000 a year and was employing one person part time to cut the grass. Now we employ 20 people full time and in excess of 100 part time, with a turnover for the group of more than £1.5 million. It started in the dining room of our house. For the first seven years it was so small that I didn't pay myself anything, even expenses,' says Strawford.

As the circuit heads towards its 50th anniversary, the team is stronger than ever. After more than 10 years working for the company, Karen stopped working to start a family with husband Graham Marshallsay. To keep up the family feel, in 1998 Graham joined the circuit as general manager and, along with Rodney Gooch, forms the key for the future management of the circuit. In the office, Doreen Miles has more than 10 years experience and more recently Emma, youngest daughter of Pat and Howard, joined the staff. She works on the press and public relations side of the business and was married in 1999 to local enthusiast Steve Burns. As a true racing enthusiast, Steve was a regular marshal at the circuit and met Emma through the sport.

Of course, Pat Strawford is a director of the companies and is central to just about everything that happens at the circuit with her customary quietly efficient manner. 'I've concentrated more on the competitors' side of things. It has been a huge part of our lives and it's been a team effort. We've been together for more than 40 years now. When Howard went rallying all those years ago, I was the navigator. Right in the early days of us being at Castle Combe I said: "Howard, I'll work with you, but I won't work for you." We do work together quite well,' says Pat.

'Without Howard, none of this would ever have happened. He just loved it from the start. Even now, he'd like to see the place looking more like a park. He's put everything into it and it's taken its toll on him. I would love to see it go on within the family. I don't think Howard will ever properly retire, as he still likes to make the decisions. He is an organiser and he is a man of his word. If you ask Howard about something, he'll tell you exactly what he thinks. You always know where you are, it's always straight and honest. Sometimes I think people hear what they don't want to hear, but that's just Howard. His bark's worse than his bite and he's got a great sense of humour,' says Pat Strawford.

For the 2000 season, work on improving the aesthetics of the circuit continued and, to celebrate the millennium, 2000 more trees and shrubs were planted at the circuit. 'I just want to achieve the smartest visitor centre in the motorsport business,' says Strawford to sum up his aspirations for the new century. His attention to detail is remarkable and Rodney Gooch well remembers an incident that is typical of Strawford's approach.

The present day control tower, complete with timekeeper's area on the top.

Photo: Paul Lawrence.

'Howard is meticulous for keeping the place neat and tidy. I hadn't been down here very long and we'd got some visitors here. We were standing somewhere around the circuit in conversation and all of a sudden, Howard walked off. I thought this was a bit strange. He got about 20 yards away and bent down to pick up this old Coke can, walked over and threw it in a rubbish bin. And that's typical of Howard, he wasn't going to leave a bit of rubbish on the ground,' recalls Gooch.

Any talk of selling the circuit is swiftly and firmly rebutted. 'There have been many rumours about me selling, particularly after I suffered a stroke. We received five offers from Brands Hatch during Nicola Foulston's time at the helm. I'm not interested in selling. I turned down £2 million from John Foulston before that and I've had many offers from others as well. The answer to all of them is no. We will leave the circuit to the girls who will own it 50/50 and Graham will manage it. I think I'll quietly fade away on the job,' says Howard Strawford with a smile.

Big grids, big crowds and close racing. Castle Combe has few rivals.

Photo: Steve Jones.

The circuit's administration centre is now a focal point in the paddock.

Photo: Paul Lawrence.

The circuit from the air in 1999. The neighbour-friendly circuit.

Photo: Steve Jones.

As ever when Castle Combe is the topic of conversation, the last words must go to the man who made it happen, Howard Strawford. 'In 1975, who would have predicted us surviving to celebrate the 50th anniversary of the circuit or dared to think that we would have funded a £200,000 improvement scheme for the configuration changes. The usage is now up from five days a year to 265 days a year. But it still won't stop me wringing my hands and saying: 'We're only just breaking even!'

Appendix 1

Outright circuit lap records for cars

Date	Driver	Car	Category	Time (speed)
07.10.50	Brian Shawe-Taylor	1488s ERA	Libre	1m20.2s (82.60mph)
06.10.51	Bob Gerard	1488s ERA	Libre	1m19.2s (83.64mph)
04.10.52	Bob Gerard	1980s ERA	Libre	1m16.8s (86.25mph)
03.10.53	Ken Wharton	1487s BRM V16	Libre	1m13.8s (89.77mph)
01.10.55	Harry Schell	2500 Vanwall	Formula 1	1m13.6s (90.00mph)
09.06.62	John Taylor	1498 Cooper	Libre	1m12.0s (92.00mph)
07.07.62	Chris Summers	4600 Cooper	Libre	1m11.2s (93.03mph)
08.09.62	Chris Summers	4600 Cooper	Libre	1m09.2s (95.72mph)
27.06.64	Hugh Dibley	2500 Brabham BT8	Sports	1m06.4s (99.76mph)
09.10.65	Chris Summers	5400 Lotus 24	Libre	1m05.2s (101.59mph)
21.05.66	Tony Lanfranchi	6000 Lola T70	Libre	1m04.6s (102.54mph)
25.05.68	Jim Moore	4727 Kincraft	Libre	1m04.4s (102.86mph)
13.07.68	Ron Fry	4727 Ford GT40	GT	1m04.4s (102.86mph)
09.05.70	Peter Gethin	4990 McLaren M10B	F5000	56.6s (117.03mph)
09.05.70	Howden Ganley	4990 McLaren M10B	F5000	56.6s (117.03mph)
07.07.84	Tony Trimmer	5700 Lola T330	Libre	55.2s (120.00mph)
06.07.85	Alo Lawler	2999 McLaren M30	Libre	54.2s (122.21mph)
25.08.97	Nigel Greensall	3500 Tyrell 022	BOSS	50.59s (130.93mph)

Circuit revised for the 1999 season

20.03.99	Mike Millard	3000 LM3000	Open Sports	1m05.61s (101.50mph)
05.04.99	Bob Light	6199 B6 Sport	GT	1m05.13s (102.25mph)
03.05.99	Bob Light	6199 B6 Sport	GT	1m04.24s (103.67mph)
31.05.99	Bob Light	6199 B6 Sport	GT	1m04.09s (103.91mph)
07.08.99	Bob Light	6199 B6 Sport	GT	1m03.94s (104.16mph)
30.08.99	Bob Light	6199 B6 Sport	GT	1m03.389s (105.07mph)

Appendix 2

Outright circuit lap records for motorcycles

Date	Driver	Machine	Category	Time (speed)
12.05.51	W G Baxter	498 Triumph	Over 350cc	1m28.4s (74.90mph)
28.07.51	H L Williams	499 Norton	500	1m23.8s (79.04mph)
06.09.52	John Surtees	499 Norton	500	1m20.8s (81.98mph)
24.07.54	John Surtees	499 Norton	Senior	1m19.2s (83.63mph)
09.07.55	John Surtees	499 Norton	Senior	1m18.0s (84.94mph)
13.07.57	Alastair King	500 Norton	Senior	1m17.2s (85.79mph)
11.07.59	Tony Godfrey	499 Norton	Unlimited	1m17.2s (85.79mph)
23.04.60	Derek Minter	500 Norton	Senior	1m15.0s (88.31mph)
21.07.62	Derek Minter	500 Norton	Senior	1m13.6s (89.99mph)
18.04.64	Tom Phillips	500 Norton	Senior	1m13.0s (90.75mph)
25.07.64	Derek Minter	500 Norton	Senior	1m12.6s (91.25mph)
05.09.64	Chris Conn	500 Norton	Senior	1m12.6s (91.25mph)
10.07.65	Derek Minter	500 Norton	Senior	1m12.2s (91.75mph)
29.04.67	Barry Randle	500 Norton	Senior	1m12.2s (91.75mph)
29.04.67	Percy Tait	500 Triumph	Senior	1m12.2s (91.75mph)
20.07.68	Dave Croxford	500 Seeley	Senior	1m12.2s (91.75mph)
18.07.70	Bryan Kemp	500 Norton	Over 500cc	1m11.4s (92.77mph)

Date	Driver	Machine	Race	Time/speed
18.07.70	Percy Tait	1000 Triumph	Over 500cc	1m11.4s 92.77mph)
24.04.71	Barry Sheene	350 Yamaha	Junior	1m10.8s (93.56mph)
24.04.71	Tony Rutter	350 Yamaha	Junior	1m10.8s (93.56mph)
29.09.84*	David Whittal-Williams	997 Suzuki		(96.05mph)
16.07.88*	Tom Blackwell	750 Suzuki	4-strokes	(97.05mph)
15.04.89	Carl Fogarty	750 Honda	1300 Star	1m04.8s (102.22mph)
28.04.90	Steve Spray	750 Norton	Superbikes	1m03.2s (104.81mph)
20.04.91	James Whitham	750 Suzuki		1m03.1s (104.97mph)
20.04.91	Ray Stringer	750 Yamaha		1m03.1s (104.97mph)
20.06.92	John Reynolds	750 Kawasaki		1m01.8s (107.18mph)
15.06.96	Graham Ward	Ducati		1m01.41s (107.86mph)

Circuit revised for the 1999 season

12.06.99	John Burgess	750 Yamaha	Open solos	1m10.42s (94.57mph)

* From 1981 to 1988 there were no records of individual lap times and the official record stood at the 1971 figure until 1989. However, by 1984, race average speeds had exceeded the previous record figure.

Appendix 3

The local champions

Formula Ford 1600 champions

1969	Bryan Sharp (Merlyn Mk11)		1986	Robert Davies (Van Diemen RF84)
1970	Peter Lamplough (Palliser WDF2)		1987	David Llewellyn (Van Diemen RF86)
1971	Mike Campbell-Cole (Merlyn Mk11A)		1988	Gavin Wills (Van Diemen RF86)
1972	Buzz Buzaglo (Elden Mk10)		1989	Gavin Wills (Van Diemen RF89)
1973	Clive Power (Dulon MP15)		1990	Nigel Jenkins (Reynard 89FF)
1974	Roger Orgee (Dulon MP15)		1991	Nigel Jenkins (Reynard 90FF)
1975	Terry Richards (Merlyn Mk11A)		1992	Bob Higgins (Reynard 91FF)
1976	David Toye (Royale RP21)		1993	Gavin Wills (Swift SC92F)
1977	David Wheeler (Royale RP21A)		1994	Gavin Wills (Swift SC92F)
1978	Mike Wallaker (Jomic Mk2)		1995	Kevin Mills (Swift SC92F)
1979	Geoff Davies (Crossle 32F)		1996	Kevin Mills (Swift SC92F)
1980	Steve Lincoln (Royale RP26)		1997	Kevin Mills (Swift SC92F)
1981	Bob Higgins (Martlet DM4)		1998	Richard Carter (Van Diemen RF92)
1982	Bob Higgins (Martlet DM4)		1999	Richard Carter (Van Diemen RF92)
1983	Bob Higgins (Royale RP29A)			
1984	Martin Cooper (Royale RP33M and Reynard 83/84FF)			
1985	Howard Lester (Reynard 83FF)			

Note: From 1969 to 1977 the championship included rounds at Llandow. In 1972 only, it also took in two rounds at Thruxton.

Special Saloon champions

1975	John Routley (Mini)
1976	Steve Harris (Mini)
1977	Reg Ward (Mini)
1978	Basil Dagge (Hillman Imp)
1979	Brian Cutting (Hillman Imp)
1980	Brian Cutting (Sunbeam Stiletto)
1981	Basil Dagge (Hillman Imp)

Note: From 1975 to 1977 the championship included rounds at Llandow. In 1975 and 1976 it was only for cars up to 1000cc, but from 1978 onwards it was for cars of all engine size.

In 1983 only, a Castle Combe Mini Championship was run over four Bank Holiday meetings and was won by Mike Fry (Mini Miglia).

Saloon Car champions

1995*	Keith Macaskill (Vauxhall Nova)
1996	Derek Wileman (Vauxhall Cavalier GSi)
1997	Ilsa Cox (Peugeot 205GTi)
1998	Russell Humphrey (Vauxhall Astra GTE)
1999	Tim Hanlon (Peugeot 205GTi)

* non-championship status.

Special GT champions

1982	Brian Cutting (Sunbeam Stiletto)
1983	Steven Roberts (Davrian Mk7)
1984	Steven Roberts (Davrian Mk7)
1985	Robin Harvey (Davrian Mk8)
1986	Brian Fisher (Skoda SR130)
1987	Brian Fisher (Skoda SR130)
1988	Brian Cutting (Sunbeam Stiletto)
1989	George Douglas (Ginetta G12) and Nigel Mustill (Ford Escort)
1990	Nigel Mustill (Ford Escort)
1991	Chris Snowdon (Davrian Mk8)
1992	Phil Lomas (Skoda-Tiga SR130)
1993	Erling Jensen (Maguire Stiletto/Skoda-Tiga SR130)
1994	Geoff Thorne (Lola T87/90)
1995	Brian Fisher (Shrike P16)
1996	Keith Messer (Lola T492H)
1997	John Robinson (Mallock Mk28)
1998	John Robinson (Mallock Mk28)
1999	John Robinson (Mallock Mk28)